"Anyone who sees their anger as a strug̲... suppress, control—or, worst of all, ignoɪ... gift of life and hope. The authors offer practical ways ... the problem and debunking the myths of anger, all with genuine acceptance and compassion. This feeling is translated into practical exercises which are easy to use, and most importantly, they really work! I have been fortunate to witness this in my own practice, even with clients with severe trauma histories and self-destructiveness. Use these techniques on your own, use them in therapy, but by all means use them and find a gentle path toward healing in the presence of anger."

—*Francis R. Abueg, Ph.D., founder and owner of TraumaResource and former associate director for research for the National Center for PTSD at the VA in Palo Alto/Menlo Park, CA*

"Empowering and compassionate, this book was written for people who struggle with anger and who find it hard to control their feelings of rage. The book describes a counterintuitive and extraordinarily insightful approach to living effectively with anger. In a lively and accessible voice, the authors describe scientifically based behavior therapy skills for letting go of our futile struggle to control anger and offer strategies to promote 'response-ability' for the one thing we can truly control: our actions. Through real-world examples, creative metaphors, and powerful experiential exercises, the reader learns to practice acceptance at even the most trying times. This book essentially is about love and freedom from unnecessary suffering—it teaches us to open up fully and to live compassionately with *what is*."

—*Laurie A. Greco, Ph.D., assistant professor in the Department of Pediatrics at Vanderbilt University Medical School and John F. Kennedy Center for Research on Human Development*

"It is possible to find a place from which you can patiently and compassionately ride a wave of anger as it rises and falls inside you and simultaneously choose to live a valued life with your hands, feet, and mouth. This book will show you how to do that with patience and compassion for yourself and others. If you regularly practice what it teaches, you will find yourself having more LIFE in your life."

—*Hank Robb, Ph.D., ABPP, past president of the American Board of Counseling Psychology*

"Looking for another way to help your clients with their anger? ACT on *Life Not on Anger* is the book for you. This book adds significantly to the therapist's options for helping clients cease battling their anger and the other vulnerable feelings it covers and instead come to terms with them as part of themselves and their lives without judgment, evaluation, and self-condemnation. This book helps people understand and accept the function of their own anger, the vital difference between feelings and actions, and the responsibility we all share to live our lives to the fullest, with respect and dignity even when we don't "feel" like it. I have already begun using this work in my own practice!"

—*L. Kevin Hamberger, Ph.D., professor of family and community medicine at the Medical College of Wisconsin*

"As an educator committed to the value of nurturing emotional intelligence in the school environment, I recommend this book particularly to students as a trustworthy life raft for navigating the endless adolescent seas of painful thoughts and confusing feelings, including one of the most burdensome and prevalent experiences of adolescence: persistent anger. As readers progress through the book, they learn— and experience—that anger need not be a provocation to destructive actions with negative consequences that are some sometimes irreversible. ACT on *Life Not on Anger'* is an excellent and life-affirming resource with clear, accessible prose, engaging illustrations, and carefully explained practical exercises. This highly readable book deserves a place in every national curriculum program."

—*Gary Powell, MA, head of German and 6th Form tutor at Trinity School in Croydon, England*

# ACT*
# on life
# not on
# anger

The New
*Acceptance & Commitment Therapy
Guide to Problem Anger

GEORG H. EIFERT, PH.D.
MATTHEW MCKAY, PH.D.
JOHN P. FORSYTH, PH.D.

New Harbinger Publications, Inc.

Publisher's Note

*This publication is designed to provide accurate and authoritative information in regard to the subject matter covered. It is sold with the understanding that the publisher is not engaged in rendering psychological, financial, legal, or other professional services. If expert assistance or counseling is needed, the services of a competent professional should be sought.*

Distributed in Canada by Raincoast Books

Copyright © 2006 by Georg H. Eifert, Matthew McKay, and John P. Forsyth
New Harbinger Publications, Inc.
5674 Shattuck Avenue
Oakland, CA 94609
www.newharbinger.com

Cover design by Amy Shoup; Acquired by Catharine Sutker; Edited by Barbara Quick; Text design by Tracy Marie Carlson

All Rights Reserved; Printed in the United States of America

Library of Congress Cataloging-in-Publication Data

Eifert, Georg H., 1952-
    ACT on life not on anger : the new acceptance and commitment therapy guide to problem anger / Georg H. Eifert, Matthew McKay, and John P. Forsyth.
        p. cm.
    Includes bibliographical references.
    ISBN-10: 1-57224-440-2 (pbk.)
    ISBN-13: 978-1-57224-440-5 (pbk.)
    1. Anger—Treatment—Popular works. 2. Cognitive therapy—Popular works. 3. Behavior therapy—Popular works. 4. Self-acceptance. 5. Commitment (Psychology) I. McKay, Matthew. II. Forsyth, John P. III. Title.
    RC569.5.A53E36 2005
    616.89'142—dc22
                                                                2005035658

FSC

Mixed Sources
Product group from well-managed forests and other controlled sources

Cert no. SW-COC-002283
www.fsc.org
© 1996 Forest Stewardship Council

12    11    10

15    14    13    12    11    10    9    8

(GHE)
To Diana, my loving wife.
She continues to teach me about anger and
its powerful antidote of patience with loving kindness.


(MM)
In memory of Peter D. Rogers.
Bon voyage, my sweet friend. Thank you for everything,
especially for teaching me to savor life.


(JPF)
Each day my wife, Celine, and my three children give me
opportunities to nurture the values of patience, compassion,
and love as vital alternatives to hurt and anger. This book is
a testimony to the lessons I have learned through them.

# Contents

Foreword     vii

Preface and Acknowledgments     xi

Introduction
A New Way of Approaching Anger     1

Chapter 1
Debunking the Myths of Anger     13

Chapter 2
Struggling with Anger Is Not a Solution     25

Chapter 3
The Heart of the Struggle                                    37


Chapter 4
Controlling Anger and Hurt Is the Problem        53


Chapter 5
How Your Mind Creates Anger                    ·    73


Chapter 6
Getting Out of the Anger Trap with Acceptance    87


Chapter 7
Practicing Mindful Acceptance                           105


Chapter 8
Taking Control of Your Life                ·                 119


Chapter 9
Facing the Flame of Anger and the Pain          135
Fueling It


Chapter 10
Commit to Take Positive Action in Your Life     155


Further Readings, References, and                 175
Other Resources

# Foreword

## ANGER, ACCEPTANCE, AND ACTION

What human beings call anger is a complex mix of thoughts, feelings, and urges toward actions pulled together into a thing called anger. Most of us have experienced the dangers of anger when it is allowed to exist entirely in that combined form. We may have hurt others in the name of anger, and in so doing we have sometimes hurt ourselves. We may have been on the receiving end of anger and have learned to fear its explosive power. We may have been obsessed by past wrongs and have allowed anger to color too many of our moments, losing contact with the opportunities for living that are here and now.

But anger is not one thing. It is many things, loosely organized by language into a whole. It is worth remembering that it's not the feeling of anger *per se* that has caused harm. Rather, the cold soup of enacted or contemplated self-righteousness or the hot energy of attacking others can easily lead to actions with negative consequences. But these need not be the core features of anger. Remember, anger is not one thing. It is many. And there are many things to do with the various "its" that reside inside anger in all of its aspects.

This book is the first effort to apply the Acceptance and Commitment Therapy (ACT, said as a word, not initials) model to anger (Hayes, Strosahl, and Wilson 1999). The authors carefully pull anger apart at the seams, showing how it is more usefully considered to be a mixture of situational cues, thoughts, feelings, impulses to act, and overt behavior. Once anger is in this disembodied form, the ACT model can be readily applied to its elements.

In this book you will be guided to do counterintuitive but and powerful new things with the feeling of anger, the thoughts that set the occasion for it, and the thoughts that trigger it. You will be able to see for yourself whether you have conflated fused the various aspects of anger needlessly and whether new approaches are possible with each aspect of anger considered individually.

Why a self-help book? It is known that many people with anger problems will avoid traditional cognitive behavioral treatments (Siddle, Jones, and Awena 2003). They may fear being on the short end of the stick; they may fear their own anger responses. This book can reach through that resistance and fear and try to touch the hearts and heads of those with anger problems.

Anger is not a clinical syndrome, and perhaps for this reason there are relatively few empirically supported approaches to it. Those that do exist show fairly limited benefits. The surprisingly ubiquitous anger-management programs are also surprisingly under-evaluated empirically. Clearly, something more is needed.

Stepping into that empirical void is a bit frightening, but the present approach is not a random walk through the issues raised by anger. This book is carefully linked to processes and ideas that are increasingly well supported empirically in more general terms.

The value of accepting emotions and defusing from thoughts has been shown in problem area after problem area. A recent review of the ACT evidence (Hayes et al., in press), showed that these processes were helpful in the areas of depression, anxiety, stress, burnout, prejudice, hallucinations, delusions, smoking, substance abuse, managing diabetes, chronic pain, and epilepsy, among others. The specific emotions and thoughts triggered by these kinds of problems run the range of possible emotions and thoughts. Given that anger overlaps with other negative emotions that have successfully been targeted, it seems to be a fairly safe bet that the same methods will be helpful in this related area. As this research program expands, we will know for sure.

There is also tantalizing research emerging from labs around the world suggesting that anger is in part a method of experiential avoidance, and that mindfulness and acceptance can be helpful. Such intuitions and early findings have turned into robust approaches in many other areas of human suffering and struggle. The work on anger seems poised for that same pattern of development.

We are not yet to àt the point of controlled research on ACT for anger, but this book is helping to make that research possible. Given the state of the evidence, however, readers need to be especially attentive to their own experience. If you are stuck in anger, this book should help give you very different things to try with this difficult collection of reactions. But no one approach will work for all. The best advice seems to be to engage in the work reflected in this book fully and honestly and to periodically consider examine your progress to see if you are happy with the results.

The authors are nationally visible experts in both anger and in ACT. Their knowledgeable hands will guide you through a counterintuitive but and innovative approach, skillfully and humanely. If you embark on this work seriously, your view of anger, its role in your life, and what you need to do with it will change, perhaps even fundamentally.

You are about to begin an interesting, exciting, and somewhat surprising journey. The destination is a valued and vital life that includes anger when you have anger, but which is not dictated, controlled, or harmed by anger feelings. Enjoy the ride, and keep your eyes wide open for the emotional and cognitive wildlife this new approach may reveal. If you stay open, you will learn a lot about how to ACT *on Life Not on Anger*.

—Steven C. Hayes
Reno, Nevada
November 2005

# Preface and Acknowledgments

There is not a human being on this earth who will go through life without emotional pain or anger. There is simply no way to get around this fact. Human beings suffer. You've suffered. We've suffered. This is the human condition. Yet we've learned that pain and anger need not destroy our lives. These emotions can be harnessed and used to enrich lives—your life!—and the human condition. ACT *on Life Not on Anger* was conceived in this spirit. Your life is what matters. The trick is to learn how to live *with* your hurt and anger and *without* damaging or restricting your relationships or possibilities. This book will show you how to do that—to reclaim the prize that is your life before it's too late.

In the process of writing this book, we suffered the tragic loss of a dear friend and colleague, Dr. Peter D. Rogers. He had every intention of contributing his wisdom to this book. Yet he did not get the chance. For a time, it looked like this tragedy might keep us from completing the book and fulfilling our intention to help people like you.

One lesson we learned from Peter's untimely death is that we all have so little time on this earth. We need to make every moment count, even when we are hurting inside. Peter learned that pain and anger could be a friend in his life, not a barrier to the life he wanted to lead. You can do this, too. Anger need not turn into suffering. You can have anger and hurt and live out your life with dignity, meaning, and purpose. Hurt and anger need not destroy what you want your life to stand for.

Moving with the pain of Peter's loss allowed us to refocus our energies on the task of writing this book. Our intention in this book is simple—to help people who have damaged their lives and the lives of others because of their hurt and anger. Our goal is to get people like you back into their lives and out of their anger trap. This life is where your legacy is—so make it count!

The ideas we express here are not just ours. We owe a debt of gratitude to the many individuals whose ideas and insights have made their way into this book. We are particularly grateful to Steven Hayes and Pema Chödrön.

Dr. Steven Hayes generously made his work and ideas available to us. In 1999, Dr. Hayes, along with his colleagues Kirk Strosahl and Kelly Wilson, published the first full-length book on Acceptance and Commitment Therapy (ACT). Several of the exercises we adapted for use with problem anger first appeared in their book.

Pema Chödrön, an American Buddhist nun, has written widely about the wisdom of meeting the strong energy of emotions such as fear and anger with patience, compassion, acceptance, and forgiveness. Her words are simple and clear, echoing the central message of this book. Her teachings about how to approach anger with mindful acceptance and compassion, and practicing patience when the anger flames are hot, embody the ACT approach to anger that we are sharing with you here. We hope that your life will be changed in profound ways by putting this approach into action in your everyday life. We have learned much from Pema Chödrön's astute knowledge and practical suggestions, and we thank her, as well as her publishers, for allowing us to draw upon her wisdom in this book.

We also thank the following professionals and the organizations that kindly gave us permission to reproduce their work: Joseph Ciarrochi and David Mercer for their artwork in chapters 4 and 10, and Joanne Dahl and the Association for Advancement of Behavior Therapy (AABT) for the life compass in chapter 8.

New Harbinger is becoming a major outlet for the dissemination of newer third-generation behavior therapies such as Acceptance and Commitment Therapy. The other two authors are grateful to Matthew McKay and all the New Harbinger staff for seeing the value of this work and its potential to alleviate a wider range of human suffering. We owe a debt of gratitude and heartfelt appreciation to Catharine Sutker of New Harbinger for her tireless energy, encouragement, and kind support as we moved ahead with this project, and likewise to Barbara Quick and Heather Mitchener for their masterful and diligent editing.

We sincerely hope you will benefit from reading this book as much as we have benefited from writing it. We particularly hope it will be useful to you in your everyday struggle with anger and other difficult emotions. Our work on this book has profoundly changed how we view the emotional pain and suffering of the people we encounter (our clients, colleagues, family, and friends). We now approach pain and suffering in ways that keep us all moving in directions we value.

Finally, we would like to thank our wives and children for giving us extra time, space, and support to complete this book. They saw the value in the work and showed a willingness to make personal sacrifices so that it could come to fruition. We truly hope they feel it was worth it—and we are committed to repaying them for their effort and faith in us!

# Introduction

# A New Way of Approaching Anger

This book offers you a way into your life and out of the anger trap based on a revolutionary new approach called Acceptance and Commitment Therapy (ACT). You will learn how to reduce the suffering that anger has caused you and others by focusing your energies on the people and experiences that matter most to you. This book will teach you how to bring acceptance and compassion to your anger, your hurts, your pains, and your thoughts—and how to extend acceptance and compassion to others in your life. Doing so will defuse the sting of anger, soften its punch, and weaken its power to get you off track from the life you want to live. You can learn to have compassion for yourself and others, and you can find out and focus on what matters most to you; you can learn to live your values.

It is possible to change your response to the triggers that make you feel angry, and to the feelings themselves. Changing those responses will change the way you behave when you're angry. Trust us that this is a brand-new approach; we're pretty sure you've never tried anything like this before.

We are going to take you down a path with your anger that will challenge you in many ways. If you read the book and do the exercises, you'll reduce your anger-related suffering. You'll increase your vitality and enhance your ability to create the kind of life you want to live, a life free of the pain of constant anger.

Learning to approach anger with acceptance and compassion will make all kinds of radical changes possible. As odd as it may sound, there are ways for you to have pain *and* find fulfilment in what you do with your life, all at the same time. Acting on and out of anger is no way to live. This is why this book is titled ACT *on Life Not on Anger.*

## FREEDOM FROM ANGER MANAGEMENT

We suspect that you have already tried to deal with your anger. Perhaps you've talked to a friend about it or perhaps you have turned to one or another self-help book. Most anger self-help books try to teach people better ways to cope with their anger. They describe people's unsuccessful struggles with anger-related thoughts and emotions. If you're like most people with problem anger, you've probably tried some of these strategies:

- Keeping the anger down when it arises

- Suppressing your anger

- Trying to calm your mind

- Changing your thoughts

- Distracting yourself

- Hitting pillows instead of people

How have such anger management techniques worked for you? We suspect they haven't worked well at all. Every person who struggles with anger knows that it is not an emotion readily controlled or coped with. Intense and action-oriented emotions such as anger are extremely difficult to change or control. The truth is that you may not be able to reduce, let alone eliminate, your anger-related thoughts and feelings.

That may sound like very bad news to you. Take heart—we are not going to take you down that same old path of more coping and anger management as a way out of your anger.

## CHOOSE A NEW APPROACH—ACT

Here's the good news: You *can* control and change how you *respond* to your anger feelings:

- You can stop trying to cope with anger feelings (if coping and other management strategies have not worked).

- You can learn to leave anger alone and simply experience it as a thought or feeling.

- You don't have to act on your anger, and it doesn't need to drive what you do. As much as you feel like yelling at your kids or the store clerk, you can learn to act differently. You can learn to watch your anger feelings and resentful thoughts and *not* do what they tell you to do.

The solution to problem anger is not to try to keep the anger down when it arises or try to get rid of it. The solution is changing your relationship with, and response to, anger thoughts and feelings. To get there, you'll need to learn how to acknowledge angry thoughts without becoming them, and without acting on them.

As we guide you in learning these skills, you will develop compassion for yourself and others. You'll also rediscover what truly matters to you; you'll focus on what you want your life to stand for and then act in ways that move you forward in your life, even if that means bringing anger or other unwanted thoughts and feelings along for the ride. This is the real prize—reclaiming your life! Looking at your life and what matters most to you is what will really help end your struggle with anger and pain.

This is not the first book on anger that attempts to help people like you develop greater compassion for yourself and others. But it is the first book that teaches you how to approach anger with compassion, so that you can live your life with meaning and purpose. Our goal is to help you spend your precious time on this earth doing what you care about deeply. Engaging in anger behavior is likely not at the top of your list. After you drop the rope in your tug-of-war with anger, you'll notice that your hands, feet, mind, and mouth are free to be put to use for the things in your life you truly care about. In the process, your life will evolve in ways that may have seemed impossible before. This book will refocus your attention and passion from your anger to the life you want to live.

## WHAT IS ACT ABOUT?

ACT is all about allowing yourself to feel what hurts while doing what works and is important to you. In a nutshell, it is about acceptance and change at the same time. If you are 100 percent willing to give this a shot, then you'll learn to accept and live with your uncontrollable anger-related thoughts and feelings *and* take charge of what you can control: your behavior.

It is only with your actions—what you do—that you move your life in the directions you want to go. When you act in ways contrary to your aspirations, you become emotionally and psychically stuck. This is a guarantee. ACT teaches you how to get unstuck and move forward by developing comfort in your own skin. You will explore new ways of living with the unpleasant thoughts and feelings that your body and mind dishes out from time to time, rather than struggling against them. Our goal is to help you understand and approach anger-related suffering in a mindful, compassionate way while pursuing what really matters to you.

The basic philosophy of ACT is similar to the well-known serenity creed: "*Accept with serenity what you cannot change, have the courage to change what you can, and develop the wisdom to know the difference.*" It is much easier to agree with the serenity creed than to do what it says. The reason is that many people simply do not know what they can or cannot change, nor how to accept and live with thoughts and feelings that hurt. As a result, they do not know how to apply this profound statement to their daily lives. Instead, they become frustrated with it. When you read this book and do the exercises, you'll learn how to make the important distinction between what you can and cannot change. This will start you on the path toward putting the serenity creed into action.

## How ACT Helps Problem Anger

Because anger can come and go very quickly, it's not necessarily harmful. Anger is only harmful and problematic if we react to feeling anger with anger behavior. ACT will help you dismantle this connection and see it for what it is—a source of needless suffering.

The ACT approach helps you experience anger without acting on it. So instead of trying to replace angry, negative thoughts with less angry, positive thoughts, we'll teach you how to watch your thoughts, all of them—gently, with dispassionate interest, and without getting caught up in them.

Learning to be a dispassionate, kind, and gentle observer of your anger thoughts and feelings may sound a bit odd. Trust us that as you learn this, you will be able to disentangle yourself from your anger thoughts and feelings. This will help you realize that you are not your anger. Your identity remains while your anger comes and goes like waves in the ocean. Knowing this will free you from the feeling that anger controls your life. You will be ready to refocus your time and energy on living the life you choose and care about.

## Three Core Steps of ACT

ACT is not just short for Acceptance and Commitment Therapy. The ACT acronym also captures nicely the three core steps or themes of this approach—**A**ccept thoughts and feelings, **C**hoose directions, and **T**ake action.

### Step 1: **A**ccept thoughts and feelings

You can accept and embrace your thoughts and feelings, particularly the unwanted ones (pain, guilt, inadequacy). Even though this may sound impossible to do, the basic idea is very simple:

- You accept and acknowledge what you already experience anyway.

- You therefore end your struggle against unwanted thoughts and feelings.

There's no need for you to attempt to eliminate or change your anger thoughts and feelings. But instead of acting upon them, you observe them with a gentle curiosity until you can ultimately let them go.

Why should you accept—and even embrace—unwanted thoughts and feelings? Mainly because old solutions in your struggle with anger have not worked and will not work. Learning to recognize what triggers your anger, and learning to observe and accept anger feelings and thoughts without acting on them, is categorically different from blow-ing up, getting even, or stuffing your anger only to act on it later by getting back at those you perceive as having wronged you. Accepting your anger thoughts and feelings is also different from the tendency to be passive when anger shows up.

Accepting anger is not about giving up, being passive, or playing the patsy. On the contrary, following this program requires a great deal of personal resolve and courage.

Once again, there is a difference between you as a person and the thoughts and feelings you have, whether about yourself or the person or event that triggered your anger. The biological function of anger is to regulate stress and pain. It's so important to recognize that stress and pain are caused by cognitive, emotional, and physical triggers. Each of these can pull you into anger and rage. That's why it's so essential for you to learn to develop a compassionate response to them. This step echoes the acceptance part of the serenity prayer.

### Step 2: Choose directions

The second step is about choosing a direction for your life. You can learn to focus your attention and energy on what really matters: your values, your goals, who you want to be in the world—the whole package. We're including several experiential exercises to help you identify what you most value in life, what you want your life to stand for. We'll hazard a guess that being an angry person 24/7 is not on your list. So this step is about helping you discover what is truly important to you and then making a choice. It is at the heart of this book: choosing to act on life, not on anger.

When you feel anger, it may seem as if your actions are auto-matic. But how you respond to anger feelings with your words, hands, and feet is actually based on a choice. When you feel anger, you can make a choice to respond with anger behavior. Or you can feel anger and respond in ways that are compassionate, caring, genuine, open, honest, and respectful—ways that will help move you in directions you want your life to go.

### Step 3: Take action

Committed action involves taking steps toward realizing your most highly valued life goals. This step is about taking charge of what you can control and changing what you can change. It involves learning to behave in ways that move you forward in the direction of your chosen values.

Taking action does not mean acting on anger or because of anger. Rather, based on your choices in step 2, you act in ways that move you in directions you want to go. You do this while accepting anger feelings that may accompany you along the way.

This is difficult, because it requires that you take a hard look at where anger is taking you and where you want to go instead. Taking action is ultimately about responsibility—or being "response*able*"— using your hands, feet, and mouth for the purposes of living the life you want to live. We'll show you how to do that.

It's natural to feel skeptical, scared, or intimidated by the prospect of making such fundamental changes in the way you behave. You may be having self-defeating thoughts right now, like, "This is too big." Don't worry about these. You cannot and need not control your thoughts or feelings. What you can control is what you do with your eye muscles and your hand muscles. Keep the book in your hands, use your eye muscles to keep on reading, and let the thoughts be what they are and do what they do. As with all thoughts and feelings, it is okay if they come, it is okay if they stay, and it is okay if they go.

# APPROACHING ANGER WITH ACCEPTANCE

When you accept a gift, you take what is offered. This is what acceptance is. Accepting anger involves recognizing and staying with your angry thoughts and feelings— making space for them—without acting on them. Acceptance doesn't mean that you believe those thoughts and feelings; it isn't about agreeing or disagreeing with them. Nor does it mean giving in to anger or being passive. You simply take note of any feelings of guilt, shame, or inadequacy—you don't argue with them or try to replace them. With acceptance there's nothing to defend. Without acceptance, you have everything to lose when anger and emotional pain show up!

Your critical, evaluative mind is the part of you that judges your thoughts and feelings. We've included several simple mindfulness, or awareness, exercises to help you learn to neutralize these judgments and the discomfort they bring.

These exercises will teach you to take a compassionate observer perspective so that you come to experience your thoughts as thoughts without reacting to them or letting them dictate your actions. We also include imagery exercises to help you notice and accept the feelings that fuel anger, such as shame, hurt, fear, failure, loss, rejection, weakness, and so on. You will see that the purpose of most anger behavior is to make those thoughts and feelings go away. Learning to recognize and stay with unwanted feelings when you have them is an important first step toward learning not to respond with anger behavior because of anger feelings.

# APPROACHING ANGER WITH COMPASSION

Anger needs an enemy to exist and grow. Meeting anger with compassion leaves anger with no room to grow. This is why compassion is so important. Compassion means that you value the happiness and welfare of others just as intensely as your own desire to be happy and lead a meaningful life.

. You may ask, "Why should I have compassion? I was hurt so badly that the other guy deserves to rot in hell." Compassion does not mean condoning or tolerating behaviors that damage you or keep you in an abusive situation. You can still protect yourself and others from harm and danger. You can still be heard. But it is better for you if you do so without harboring ill will toward those people. Holding on to your anger keeps it alive, even when you don't act on it. This will not only keep you feeling tense and unhappy, but it will also give anger room to spill over and affect just about every part of your life that you care about: work, family, friends, health, and recreation. Is this what you want?

Responsibility for your anger behavior is just the same as responsibility for the other ways in which you choose to live your life: the choice begins with you and is ultimately about you. We cannot guarantee that other people will meet your compassion with compassion. But acting on anger only fosters more negative energy; anger behavior rarely if ever yields compassion. Here's the one guarantee we can give you if you put this program into action: you will act in ways that will nurture your sense of value and dignity. If this matters to you, then stick with the program!

## APPROACHING ANGER WITH GENTLE AWARENESS

Through the mindfulness exercises in chapter 7, you will learn to develop awareness of what you are experiencing in the present moment. The exercises will help you experience that you are not your thoughts or feelings; you are not your anger. They all are part of you, but they are not *you*. Your experience is not something you need to control or run away from, or act on at all.

If you've struggled with anger, you probably already know that with anger comes a tendency to judge yourself and others. Judging only feeds anger and gets us nowhere. This is why we suggest a different approach, using exercises to build up your capacity for compassion by acknowledging and accepting your anger, along with the pain, fear, and judgments about yourself and others that drive it. The purpose of these exercises is to set the stage for gradually replacing old, habitual, automatic ways of behaving (such as blowing up) with new, flexible, and intentional ways of behaving—ways that you consciously choose.

You will learn to notice and observe the temporary feelings that arise in your mind and body with compassion, with gentle kindness, and without acting on them or because of them.

Anger and judgment are fleeting parts of you that, although recurrent, come and go like clouds in the sky, the changing seasons, and so on. For example, Mike's wife promised to pick up the kids but she didn't do it. Enraged, Mike had the thought, "She only cares about her schedule and doesn't give a damn about my time. I'm really going to tell her off when she gets home." Mike couldn't do anything about the rage arising in his body or the vengeful thoughts popping into his mind at the time. Yet, he had lots of options when it came to how he responded to them and what he decided to do about them. Mike eventually learned to simply watch these feelings and thoughts, recognize them as feelings and thoughts, and absolutely *not* follow through on them. This opened up a range of choices for Mike to act differently.

You can also learn to make life-affirming choices rather than letting your anger feelings coerce you into destructive choices. And guess who's in charge then: you!

## DON'T BELIEVE US OR YOUR MIND—TRUST YOUR EXPERIENCE!

We'll do our best to explain what we know about anger. Yet words are only words unless you experience their meaning. Simply learning about anger with your head, without taking steps to put your learning into action, is a dead end. You know as much from your own personal experience. Studies have shown over and over that learning is most effective when people experience what they learn about. So the challenge is to apply what you learn from this book in your daily life. This will take hard work and commitment.

Here's an important consideration: You don't need to believe what we say or understand every point we make. Some of what you read in this book is going to sound quite strange at first, perhaps even silly and bizarre. We guarantee that your mind will throw many arguments at you why this or that sounds impossible, is too difficult, or doesn't make any sense. When such thoughts occur, thank your mind for each of them and then move on. You need not argue with your mind or try to convince yourself of anything. The only things we ask are that you try to stay open to a new way of relating to anger and new experiences; that you do the exercises; and that you check out whether, over time, they start working for you. Then trust that experience, and let your mind do its thing.

This is why each chapter includes a number of exercises. The exercises are the most important parts of this book. They help you experience what works and what doesn't. Exercises bring to life in a personal way what you have learned. Some of them help you feel what hurts, what underlies your anger, and how you can experience anger without acting on it. Understanding this logically is helpful, but only experiencing it will make a difference in your life. This book will help you and work for you—but only if you work *with* it.

How can you do that? Make reading a priority in your schedule. Commit to a reasonable amount of time you can set aside to read this book and practice the exercises. We recommend that you not read several chapters of this book all at once. Doing so will make it difficult for you to put the concepts into action. You need to think about the concepts presented here—let them percolate. You need to allow yourself time to put the concepts into practice. This will take time.

Put taking care of yourself on your to-do list every day. Pace your reading so that you read and practice the concepts in one chapter every week. We've structured the chapters to be read this way for the simple reason that change and learning any new skill take time. Reading one chapter of this book every week is a great way to take care of yourself, as is doing the exercises every day. Don't move on until you've spent sufficient time with the material in each chapter to allow you to put the concepts into action.

Commitment is a central component of any effort to change one's life. Are you ready for that commitment when it comes to your anger? Are you willing to learn another way to approach your anger thoughts and feelings? If you are, you can take control over your actions and commit to move in life directions you truly value. Without commitment to action—if you don't complete the exercises— nothing much is going to change in your life. As Steven Hayes and his colleagues wrote, "If you always do what you always did, you will always get what you always got!" (1999, p. 235). Just reading this book without doing anything new is a surefire way to continue to get what you've always got.

## BEGIN YOUR JOURNEY

In the end, you control the direction you want your life to take—that is your choice. Reading this book—and internalizing what you learn— is part of this process. But there's no book on the planet, nor any person, who can make you live your life in a certain way. It will be up to you to put what you learn into action and make the changes you need to make. This book is designed to help you get something different by doing something different! As you commit to putting your values into action, the quality of your life, and the quality of life of those around you, will begin to improve.

There is a Buddhist saying that the journey of a thousand miles begins with one step. By selecting and reading this book, you have taken that first step on your journey out of your anger trap and into a new life. Congratulations! Now keep moving forward. Living according to your values is a lifelong pursuit. On your journey, you will continuously learn, progress, and see life in a way that you may never have experienced before. This book is a kind of travel guide. Use the information here to help you decide where you want to go.

# Chapter 1

# Debunking the Myths of Anger

*At the moment you become angry, you tend to believe
that your misery has been created by another person.
You blame him or her for all of your suffering. By
looking deeply, you may realize that the seed of anger
in you is the main cause of your suffering.*

—Thich Nhat Hanh

Have you sometimes felt that the feeling of anger is inevitable and that
you'd better find a way to let off steam before you burst into aggression? Have you been to a therapist who advised you to stop holding
your anger in? Have you ever gotten angry and had a friend reassure

you that it's good to get it all out? Have you ever found yourself in situations thinking such thoughts as "If I hadn't gotten angry and fought back, this guy would have continued to walk all over me" or "If they had treated me with respect, I wouldn't have yelled at them"? These are all common beliefs and misconceptions about anger—even some mental health professionals accept them. Yet, none of them are true. Each is based on a myth. They are harmful because they keep you and others like you stuck in self-destructive patterns. Let us introduce you to the five basic myths of anger:

Myth 1: Anger and aggression are instinctual to humans.

Myth 2: Frustration inevitably leads to aggression.

Myth 3: Venting your anger is healthy.

Myth 4: Anger is always helpful.

Myth 5: A person's anger is caused by others.

All myths of anger justify the expression of anger and aggressive behavior. Each myth suggests that anger is an inevitable part of being human. This inevitability makes anger seem inescapable—and perhaps even gives it value as a human attribute. Pop psychology articles and talk shows play into this misperception by encouraging and even praising the expression of anger, affirming its inevitability, and stressing the value of managing it. Anger, we are told, is part of our nature. All of us have heard, in one form or another, that expressing anger—letting it all out—is the royal road to physical and mental health.

You may already sense from your own experience that there is something wrong with this set of assumptions. Has letting anger out really worked for you? Has it helped you live the life you want, or has it brought ruin to important areas of your life? Letting anger out does not work for most of us, and it probably has caused you—and others in your life—a lot of pain.

Through our work and the research of others, we've come to believe that the expression of anger isn't unavoidable or necessary, and it certainly isn't helpful. Let's briefly examine each of the five myths one by one.

# MYTH 1: ANGER AND AGGRESSION ARE INSTINCTUAL TO HUMANS

The idea that humans are endowed with a basic instinct for anger and aggression has been used to explain just about everything from marital quarrels to global warfare. The thinking here is that innate biological pressures can push people past some built-in anger threshold. Even the American Psychological Association (APA) contributes to keeping this view alive:

> The instinctive, natural way to express anger is to respond aggressively. Anger is a natural, adaptive response to threats; it inspires powerful, often aggressive, feelings and behaviors, which allow us to fight and defend ourselves when we are attacked. A certain amount of anger, therefore, is necessary to our survival. (APA 2005)

## We Thrive on Cooperation and Nurturing

Though these ideas make some intuitive sense—seemingly accounting for the often explosive and senseless nature of rage and aggression—they are fundamentally flawed for one main reason: Successful evolution is based on cooperation, not destructive conflict and aggression. Even primates fight in a ritualized way. They do so to preserve the species, not to kill their adversaries. More commonly, acts of violence across species tend to occur in defense of the group, typically for purposes of protecting territory or resources.

When people feel threatened, it is natural for them to feel anger. But this feeling does not justify anger behavior. In fact, in the context of cooperation and promotion of the greater good, acts of violence, aggression, hate, and envy are nonsensical. As human beings, we have always lived in small bands of closely related members who have nurtured and helped rather than destroyed each other. Such actions promote growth and survival. Violence directed toward one's own group or kin undermines the survival and overall welfare of the group and those who belong to it.

Look at the fundamental pattern of our existence from birth to old age: we constantly seek nurture, and thrive when we're nurtured. Humans and other primates deprived of basic nurturing fail to thrive.

Maybe the fundamental nature of human beings is gentleness and kindness—although we admit that watching the nightly news can make you wonder!

### Anger Is Not in Our Genes

After considering all the available evidence at a conference in 1986, a group of twenty distinguished behavioral scientists concluded that there is no scientific evidence to support the belief that humans are innately aggressive. Waging war and other violent behavior is not genetically programmed into our human nature. Except for rare pathologies, genes do not produce individuals predisposed to violence. There is nothing in our brain setup that compels us to act violently. In fact, our evolutionary history has favored our ability to cooperate.

### Violence Doesn't Always Stem from Anger

We know that lots of aggression occurs without any feelings of anger. Violence (even killing) can occur for a number of reasons that have nothing to do with feeling angry. A hunter killing an animal for food typically kills without feeling anger. A prizefighter aims to hit another fighter without feeling angry, because such feelings are likely to mar his ability to score punches. Soldiers in the military train to kill other human beings, but they may experience guilt and sorrow more often than anger. You can feel angry without acting that anger out in violent ways. In fact, anger feelings seem to be followed by aggressive behavior only about 10 percent of the time (DeAngelis 2003).

Aggressive behavior is one among many choices you can make when you experience anger. You can learn to make other choices.

## MYTH 2: FRUSTRATION INEVITABLY LEADS TO AGGRESSION

The view that frustration leads to aggression was popularized by Sigmund Freud, who believed that individuals are born with an innate aggressive instinct. He also thought that blocking or frustrating the instinct for aggression only leads to it being redirected somewhere else. So, when you perceive whatever makes you angry as being too risky to attack (for example, your boss), you redirect or displace your anger on someone or something that's less risky or threatening. Thus, you may displace aggression toward your boss by picking a fight with one of your subordinates, yelling at your children, smashing something, or even kicking your dog.

The idea that frustration leads to aggression received quite a bit of research support early on in the 1950s and 1960s. We now know, however, that aggression is not the only behavior that can follow frustration and hurt. In fact, there are many instances in other cultures, including those that are Westernized, where frustration does not invariably lead to aggressive behavior. For instance, many Tibetan people were abruptly displaced from their homeland after the Chinese invaded Tibet in 1952. Most of these individuals now live in exile. Yet, despite the hardship they endured, the Tibetans have largely refrained from aggressive action toward the Chinese. In fact, their leaders shun violence and consistently encourage their people to practice nonviolence and compassionate understanding. The same posture is true of the people of Bali. Even in Westernized cultures, you will find that people respond in a variety of ways to frustration. Some people will curse, hit, or kick something after losing money in a vending machine. Others will write down the name and address of the vending company and request a refund by mail. Many more people will simply shrug their shoulders and walk away.

Still, the persistence of the frustration-leads-to-aggression myth is surprising. An unfortunate consequences of this lingering misperception is that people use it to explain and excuse the anger they express when they don't get what they want. Frustration is far too often seen as a direct route to provoking anger and aggression, and anger is rationalized as an automatic and natural response. Many people assume that anger is the only possible way to respond when things go wrong and they feel frustrated. This myth leads people to buy into the idea that they have no choice about how they respond.

The reality, though, is that there are always choices; anger is only one of several possible responses to frustration. In this book we offer you a whole new range of choices and ways to respond when you feel anger and experience frustration.

# MYTH 3: VENTING YOUR ANGER IS HEALTHY

The idea that venting anger to let off steam is necessary and helpful has become part of popular culture. It originates from what we see as misunderstood statements by Sigmund Freud and his followers.

The myth is that frustration can build up over time; that it must be released one way or the other. Bottled-up, unexpressed anger supposedly festers in your mind and body, creating both physical and emotional disease and poisoning relationships at work, school, and play, in love, in all areas of life itself (Bry 1976). The basic cure, then, is to express your anger—letting it all out—to cleanse and purify your body and mind. This cleansing is sometimes referred to as "catharsis," which literally means "purging." It is supposed to clear the air, resulting in healthier and happier communication with the people around you, giving you a good, clean feeling, and increasing your self-esteem.

It took many years of research to finally put the venting idea to rest. Blowing off steam is not beneficial. One of the most renowned anger researchers, Carol Tavris (1989), rightly observed that the people who are most prone to vent their rage simply get more rather than less angry when they do so. And those at the receiving end of anger outbursts get angry too. You may have noticed this yourself in your interactions with colleagues, with friends, or perhaps with your partner or children at home. It all starts with some precipitating event, which is followed by an angry outburst, shouting, screaming, or crying; a crescendo (perhaps even including physical violence); exhaustion and finally withdrawal and/or eventually an apology. Have you noticed how this cycle can be replayed over and over with no catharsis or decrease in your overall level of anger?

When anger is let out, it is typically met with anger right back. This is what venting anger does. Negative energy breeds more negative energy. Behavior such as yelling or even talking out an emotion doesn't reduce anger feelings. What actually happens is that you are rehearsing more of the same. Punching a pillow while thinking of someone you dislike is rehearsing punching the person. Numerous studies have shown as much: venting anger typically serves to "freeze" a hostile attitude or opinion (Tavris 1989). You probably know from your own experience that venting does not make hostile feelings go away. Instead, they tend to stick around longer and haunt you.

The bottom line is that the popular remedy for anger, venting it by letting it all out, is really worse than useless. Expressing anger does not reduce anger. Instead, it functions to make you even angrier. Venting also solidifies an angry attitude and state of mind, escalates anger and aggression, and does nothing to help you (or the recipient of your anger) resolve the situation. Buying into the idea that letting it all out somehow purifies you is also dangerous because people can use it as a license to hurt others. You may have even done this yourself.

Sometimes people do feel relieved after they vent their anger. You may have experienced this, too. Yet numerous research studies have found that such relief is not a natural consequence of anger, but rather a learned reaction (for example, Hokanson 1970). Some people have learned to feel relief following expression of anger, just as other people learn to feel shame or increased compassion after venting. This learning involves making an erroneous connection between acting out anger and the calm most people return to after anger has passed. This connection is erroneous because people would have felt calmer and better anyway after a while, even without acting out their anger. The good news is that you can learn new responses and change how you respond to your anger feelings. Viewed this way, your response to anger feelings with anger actions becomes a choice rather than an inevitability. Acting on anger is not inevitable, instinctual, or something you need to keep doing.

## MYTH 4: ANGER IS ALWAYS HELPFUL

Because it triggers a surge of adrenaline, anger can mobilize you to defend yourself or escape when you are physically threatened or attacked. This is called the fight-or-flight response. Anger can help you set appropriate limits and overcome any fear you may have about asserting your needs. Anger is also a common intermediate step in the healing process following sexual or physical abuse. Yet even in those difficult situations, anger ceases to be beneficial when the abused person is unable to let go of it. Consuming anger can actually leave you stuck and unable to move beyond your pain.

Anger is beneficial when it serves as a warning signal that something is wrong. It can increase your sense of control and certainty, and—most importantly—prepare you for action (Lerner and Keltner 2001). The type of anger and pain we are talking about here involves situations in which people have clearly been hurt or are at risk of being harmed. Their pain is both an impetus and a catalyst for positive action to protect themselves or others from further harm.

Anger in such circumstances isn't fueled by a stance of general hostility. Instead, it is an appropriate reaction to a real threat or danger. Fear is likewise an appropriate emotion upon seeing an approaching gang of thugs while walking alone on a city street at night. When the danger passes, so does the fear. Constructive anger can function in much the same way. But when anger spills over into other life situations where it is uncalled for, it can become a problem for you. Take a moment to think about how often your anger occurs in response to situations that have little or no chance of causing you physical injury or risk of death. This probably happens frequently, right?

Anger fueled by hostility (as distinct from anger that serves as a warning) is anger in its most harmful form. Hostility or cynical anger is a state of mind of ill will fueled by strong judgments about yourself and other people. This type of cynical or hostile anger, let alone hatred, is never useful or helpful. It can easily lead to aggressive behavior, verbal or otherwise. It is toxic in that it ultimately damages your mind and body.

Researchers found evidence seemingly showing that all anger is bad for your health, particularly for your heart (see Friedman 1992). Now, half a century and many studies later, convincing medical and psychological research shows that hostile anger is the only type of anger that is truly harmful to you, both physically and psychologically. A recent study was able to demonstrate exactly how hostility increases your risk of developing cardiovascular disease by weakening the immune system. The critical toxic element is an attitude of ill will toward others and the tendency to cause physical harm and express aggression toward others (Suarez, Lewis, and Kuhn 2003).

Hostile anger damages areas of your life you care about, harming other people in your orbit at the same time that it harms you. A study by Smith and Gallo (1999), for instance, showed that hostile angry people are not only at greater risk of developing cardiovascular disease, but their nonangry spouses are put at greater risk as well!

# MYTH 5: A PERSON'S ANGER IS CAUSED BY OTHERS

In our clinical practice, we consistently notice that angry clients come into therapy with one or more reasons to explain and justify why they are so angry. Though the stories differ, the message is the same: "My anger is caused by someone else or something else. I'm not to blame.

When you're in pain, it's logical to ask yourself, "Who did this to me; who's responsible?" As soon as you decide that someone else is responsible for your hurt or physical tension, the focus shifts from you to them. You can then feel justified in discharging your pain and hurt with anger directed toward those you believe to be responsible for it.

Anger is triggered by people and events outside your control. How you react to your anger thoughts and feelings is up to you, though. By shifting the blame to others, you rob yourself of the opportunity to make changes in your behavior—and you keep yourself stuck in a cycle of anger behavior triggered by anger feelings.

# WHY ARE THESE MYTHS SO PERSISTENT?

The belief that anger is caused by external factors, and that anger-inspired aggression is unavoidable, is psychologically attractive for many people. It allows them to excuse and justify acts of aggression by suggesting that they had little choice in the matter. Buying into any of the anger myths cements the relation between anger feelings and anger behavior. It makes anger behavior seem natural and even healthy.

Yet the relation is neither natural nor healthy. All of the myths serve to keep you thinking that there is nothing you can do, that you're doomed, with no space to move and make other choices. In this book, we will help you experience the possibility of separating anger *feelings* from anger *behaviors*. What you do in response to anger feelings is determined far more by choice than by your nature.

# TAKING CHARGE: ASSERTING PERSONAL RESPONSE-ABILITY IN YOUR LIFE

So the question is, Who really is responsible when anger and hurt show up? The perception that someone has caused your pain turns you into a victim. You see yourself as threatened, under siege by another person's wrongdoings. When someone else is responsible, you can turn your focus away from your pain. You can concentrate on listing the sins perpetrated against you and the injustices that you have suffered—and for a while you may even feel better.

But let's pause for a moment here and ask: Has this relief ever lasted? Or has it instead led to more anger, tension, and suffering? How has blaming worked for you? Has blaming and blowing up moved you closer to leading the life you want to live? Could it be that anger behavior is more about the person having it (you) than about the person who seems to trigger it?

You may be wondering whether we are about to turn on you and tell you something like "It's not other people or other things that make you angry. It's you—only you are responsible for how you feel." Relax! We're not about to do that, simply because blaming and beating up on yourself is no more helpful than blaming and beating up on others. Blaming is negative energy that puts you and others down. It feeds anger, tends to inflict needless harm, and keeps the anger cycle going. There are alternatives to this cycle, and two of them stand out: understanding and compassion.

Is it possible that the whole process of assigning blame doesn't work—that the answer to your question about who's responsible can't be found by finding someone to blame? Perhaps it might help to put the question in a slightly different way: Who is *response-able*? Who is truly *able* to respond when anger shows up? Who can choose to respond differently? Who has the power to change things in your life? Like it says in the Cole Porter song, "You, you, you!"

Think about what you can really control in your life. What is really important to you, and what do you want to live for? Honest answers to such questions are likely to point you in new directions.

Ultimately, the idea of response-ability is a very positive and liberating one. It begins by recognizing that it is difficult, if not impossible, to control your anger thoughts and feelings—as much as you may want to. The next part involves acknowledging what you can control—

namely, what you do with your hands, feet, and mouth when anger shows up. This issue of control is an important one, and we'll discus it thoroughly in chapter 4.

Responsibility for anger behavior begins with you. It is time to face up to that reality. This is good news, because your behavior is something you can control—even though it may feel hard to control what you do when anger thoughts and feelings seem to possess you. For the moment, ask yourself these questions:

- Where has anger behavior gotten me, and what have I gained from it?

- How much energy have I been tying up in managing my anger feelings?

- Do I have the courage to take a stand and respond differently to anger feelings?

## THE TAKE-HOME MESSAGE

Anger has cost you dearly in many domains of your life. The myths suggesting that anger is biologically inevitable and helpful, and that anger venting is useful, are all wrong. Buying into these myths works against you. The principle of response-ability suggests a new and different posture with respect to your anger and your life. This posture has the power to pull the rug out from underneath your anger, because it focuses on what is important to you and what you can do and change. It weakens the tendency to point the finger at others. It also weakens your insistence that others should change what they do first. The ACT approach puts you in charge.

# WEEK I

## Anger is neither instinctual nor caused by others

**Point to ponder:** By taking response-ability for my anger, I can take charge of my life.

**Questions to consider:** What myths of anger have I bought into to justify my behavior? Have I let anger control my life? Am I willing to take response-ability for what I do about my anger and with my life?

# Chapter 2

# Struggling with Anger Is Not a Solution

*Clinical experience has shown that, ironically, it is often the patient's very attempts to solve the problem that, in fact, maintain it. The attempted solution becomes the true problem.*

—Giorgio Nardone and Paul Watzlawick

You want to change your anger. Perhaps your wish to change follows some event where you lost control. Or perhaps you've struggled a long time, looking desperately for a way to stop the damage anger does to your relationships and your life. You've reached this moment—reading this book—because you no longer want be trapped in your old anger responses.

# ASSESSING THE COSTS OF ANGER

The struggle with anger has cost you—in the coin of energy, of deep and painful regret, of damage to your closest bonds. You sense that your efforts at anger control—and all the ways those efforts have failed—have left a deep mark on you.

You probably already have a pretty good idea how much responding with anger has cost you in the various areas of your life. Have you experienced broken and strained relationships? Sickness and poor health? Excessive stress? Difficulties at school or work? Problems with alcohol or other substances? There may also be other costs that are less obvious, or that you choose not to think about.

The following exercise on assessing the costs of anger can help you examine exactly what anger has cost you in your life. This will also give you a better idea of what you have missed out on by responding to anger feelings with anger behavior.

You may already have an idea that something is wrong. This is a good starting point. The difficult work is facing exactly what is wrong and coming to terms with what anger has cost you. You will see that we are asking you to look at your personal experience with anger. Nobody is more of an expert about your experience than you. Are you willing to get started? If so, then get a pen and a separate piece of paper. Let's begin.

## ASSESSING THE COST OF YOUR ANGER

### 1. Interpersonal Costs

Summarize the effects of anger on your relationships. Have friendships changed or been lost? Have family members been alienated? Do they avoid you, or do you avoid them? Have you lost a marriage or romantic relationship due to anger?

### 2. Career Costs

Summarize the effects of anger on your career. Have you ever quit or been fired from a job because of anger? This includes overt anger as well as passive aggression—slacking off, being late, being less productive, bad-mouthing people, gossip, and so on. Have coworkers ever been alienated by your anger? Has your anger affected your school career (relationships with teachers, administrators)?

### 3. Health Costs

Describe the effects of anger on your health. There is a lot of research showing that anger stresses your body. Do you have any physical problems that could be stress related? Do you tend to get sick often? Do you experience physical symptoms during or after anger episodes (such as chest pain, muscle tension, upset stomach, headache)? Do you sometimes ruminate and stew over anger to the point of feeling sick or keyed up or having insomnia?

### 4. Energy Costs

Outline how anger has affected your energy. Does your anger sometimes exhaust you? Have you put time and energy into disappointing efforts at control? Have your attempts to manage anger left you feeling discouraged, fatigued, or worn out?

### 5. Emotional Costs

What has anger cost you emotionally? How much guilt do you carry for damage done by your anger? How do regrets about your anger episodes affect you emotionally? Are you affected by relationship losses due to anger? Do you suffer depression or hopelessness in the wake of your anger?

## EXAMPLE ASSESSMENT

Here's how Rachel, an insurance claims adjuster, completed her assessment of the costs of her anger:

### 1. Interpersonal Costs

*Mom and I fight, and then we don't talk for months. Two relationships with boyfriends got screwed up because of fighting. Rod and Jeanine—both friendships blew up in a fight. Quit the Unitarian singles group because of a* hassle with Bill (the leader). Tend to get angry when I'm just starting to date someone and they don't do things like I expect.

## 2.  Career Costs

Lost three jobs because of hassles with a boss. Blew a promotion because I told Carl (old boss) he was a cheap shit. Hassles with Annie made life shit at the job I had before that.

## 3.  Health Costs

Upset stomach when I stayed pissed for a while. Getting sick a lot. (Does anger lower resistance?) I worry about my heart sometimes, because it beats hard the whole time I'm angry.

## 4.  Energy Costs

I'm always trying to watch myself, trying not to get into it with people who piss me off. I guess that's tiring. The anger kind of energizes me and then I crash later. It's like I'm on something, but it wears off and I go down. I get bummed after I get into it with someone— much later I kick myself for losing control.

## 5.  Emotional Costs

Loneliness—there'd be more people in my life if I didn't get angry. Maybe I'd have a boyfriend if little stuff didn't get me so pissed off. Depression, disappointment, things not turning out and all that shit. Thinking about Lou—screwing up a good thing. I think about him a lot.

Completing your assessment of the costs of your anger is a crucial first step in honestly facing how anger has damaged you and continues to do so. But it has a further purpose. It's important that you recognize and feel the effects of your anger despite all your efforts, promises, and resolutions to change it. So let's start there.

# YOUR ANGER MANAGEMENT HISTORY

In the previous exercise, you experienced the costs associated with your anger. Many of these costs probably led you to do this or that to avoid them in the future. For instance, you may have blamed yourself or others for your hurt. You may have insisted on your being right and others being wrong. You may have blown up and yelled at people. Have these strategies made you less angry and happier with your life? Have they moved you in directions you want your life to take? Here, we want you to experience with what you have done about your anger and how well that's worked for you. You need to feel this in your heart and not just understand it in your mind. Why might this be?

The simple and honest answer is that we don't want you to go on doing more of the same, especially when old anger management strategies haven't worked for you. Successful anger transformation begins with facing—openly and honestly—each attempt at anger management, each past strategy, and seeing how it has worked. This isn't easy, which is why we've designed an exercise to help you identify clearly what hasn't worked for you.

## TAKING STOCK OF YOUR ANGER MANAGEMENT HISTORY

Right now, we'd like you to look back at your past attempts to manage and control anger. This exercise will help you organize your memories across different situations and relationships. The exercise is a bit long, so we'll do it in two parts. The left-hand column of the grid lists categories of people who might trigger anger. If you've experienced anger in relation to one or another such person in your life, fill in the corresponding boxes in columns 2 and 3 (or use a separate piece of paper for your answers). You can skip the people triggers that don't apply to you.

In column 2 you should describe how you cope to manage and control your anger when it's ignited. What do you do with the feeling? Do you try to keep it from erupting? Do you push it down? Do you talk about it? Do you tell yourself not to react? Do you try to relax? Do you reach for a drink? Do you beat yourself up for past episodes with lots of negative self-talk? Do you promise people you're going to change?

In column 3, go ahead and describe the outcome of your anger management efforts. Have you succeeded in reducing your anger feelings? Have you succeeded in controlling your aggressive behavior? Have you been able to protect your relationships? Have you dealt with triggering feelings (shame, guilt, stress, frustration) in ways that don't ignite anger? Think about both the short term and the long term as you respond to these questions. Most importantly, what have you traded in or lost because of anger management and control efforts? Examples could be lost time or energy, frustration, missed opportunities, or diminished relationships or activities that you might enjoy or care about. Some of these losses may be similar to the costs you outlined in the previous exercise.

| People triggers | Coping strategy (my behaviors) | Outcome |
|---|---|---|
| Parents | | |
| Other family members | | |
| Supervisors | | |
| Coworkers/subordinates | | |
| Friends | | |
| Partner/spouse | | |
| Other drivers | | |

When doing an exercise like this, it can sometimes be helpful to read how another person filled it out. Take a look at the notes that Andy, a body shop foreman, made on his anger management history exercise.

| People triggers | Coping strategies (my behaviors) | Outcome |
|---|---|---|
| My father criticized me. | I act tough, withdraw, and stay away from him. | No relationship. Talk at Xmas on the phone. |
| My sister puts me down. | I tell her nothing about myself, give her no ammo. | No relationship. Feel alone. |
| Boss criticizes my work. | Get cold, distant, tell him he doesn't know what he's talking about. | Used to be friends. Now he doesn't invite me to do things anymore. |
| Coworkers give me sloppy work. | Only give them written feedback to avoid blowing up. | People resent my notes, make jokes about me. |
| Friends don't keep promises or aren't on time. | I don't say anything and pretend I'm okay about it. | I withdraw and stop calling them. Feel disgusted. Think about it for long time. |
| Girlfriend disses or pressures me. | I get sarcastic, or withdraw and stuff it. | Feel resentful and more distant; lose sexual interest. |
| Other drivers cutting me off. | I seethe. Shout at them in my car; lay on the horn. | Get the finger a lot from other drivers. Two speeding tickets in the past year. |

In the first part of this exercise we looked at people who might trigger your anger. In the second part, you'll identify feelings that might trigger your anger. Examples of such feelings are listed in the left-hand column. If you've experienced anger in response to any of the feelings listed, fill in the corresponding boxes in columns 2 and 3. Again, you can skip the triggers that don't apply to you.

Emotional triggers are often less obvious than people triggers, so you may find it harder to identify them. Pay special attention to feelings you don't like or that have an unpleasant quality to them. As before, in column 2 you should describe what attempts you make to manage and control anger when it's ignited. In column 3, describe the outcome of your anger management efforts. Again, focus on what you've traded in or lost because of anger management and control efforts. Some of these may be similar to the costs you described previously.

You can use a separate piece of paper for your answers if they won't fit easily on the chart.

| Emotional triggers | Coping strategies (my behaviors) | Outcome |
|---|---|---|
| Frustrated | | |
| Ashamed/guilty | | |
| Stressed | | |
| Afraid | | |
| Controlled | | |
| Disappointed | | |
| Threatened | | |

Here's how Andy filled in this part of the exercise. Notice that he customized the feelings categories to more closely reflect his personal situation.

| Emotional triggers | Coping strategies (my behaviors) | Outcome |
|---|---|---|
| Frustrated | I try to keep frustration to myself or come up with a reason for why things have gone wrong. | Sometimes I hit something (like the wall) to release my frustration. |
| Ashamed/guilty after screwing up | Try to say nothing and just fight for control of how I feel. | End up feeling worse for it; push people away and they resent me. |
| Feeling stressed when rushing or late | Try to stay controlled and keep my voice calm. | Eventually lose it; blow up if slightest thing goes wrong. |
| Feeling controlled by my girlfriend | I get sarcastic and withdraw. | Feel resentful, distant, "not there." We fight about this. |

When Andy reviewed this exercise, it was clear that his usual coping strategies (being cold, distant, controlled, withdrawn, sarcastic, or silent) weren't working. That's because the outcome was usually to get so distant from others that relationships were damaged or lost.

After completing the anger management history exercise, we'd like you to take stock of what you've learned. Have your efforts to control anger worked? Have you kept relationships safe from the corrosive effects of your anger? Have all your efforts to manage rage still ended in episodes of lashing out? Have your efforts to keep anger feelings down actually kept them down? Or has anger continued to eat at you?

If you're like a lot of people, nothing you've done to control anger has really worked. You keep doing things you regret. You keep damaging the ones you need and love. And you keep trading in more and more of your life flexibility in an effort to get a handle on your anger.

What does your heart, your gut, tell you about your history with anger? In your heart, do you feel sick about it? Helpless? Hopeless? What does your experience tell you about your response to anger? Take a moment to take stock.

Anger is a powerful feeling that can sweep away your strongest resolve. Despite your efforts to manage and control anger, you still pay for it. You keep feeling bad about yourself and those who trigger your anger. You want to change, but no amount of remorse or effort seems to stem the force of your ignited rage. This is not a time to apply more willpower, either. You've already been down that road. We can tell you this much: more willpower is not the solution. You only need to be willing to adopt a different strategy—take a different path.

## I'M STUCK AND AT MY WITS' END; NOW WHAT?

Feeling stuck and at your wits' end is an important moment, because there is a lesson here that can change your life. Knowing in your mind and heart—with absolute certainty—that the things you've done because of anger and to manage anger don't work is the first step on a new road. Admitting and accepting that your anger feelings are stronger than your efforts to stop them creates a paradoxical new freedom. You can do something new— because all your old, tried-and-true ways to cope aren't working and will not work.

This is a watershed. It starts with acknowledging that your experience is your best guide. What does that experience with anger tell you? Go ahead and look back at your responses to the earlier exercises. The situation probably looks hopeless. Yet there is hope, because there is another way. Hope starts with giving up on and stopping all your old anger management and control efforts. They haven't worked and will not work in the future. They've kept you trapped with a false belief that control is possible, that anger management is possible, and, perhaps, if you work harder at it or trade in a little more of your life, things will get better. Your experience tells you this isn't so: so as long as you keep trying, you keep failing.

Everything you will learn here rests on this understanding: All the old strategies for *managing* anger lead to a dead end. They hurt you. This is why you need to stop them. Your experience tells you as much. It is time to let go of old, unworkable strategies.

## THE TAKE-HOME MESSAGE

There is a way out of the anger trap. You can liberate yourself from the struggle. But the answer lies in a place you've never looked before. It will be difficult, it will feel backwards, it will mean heading *toward* what you instinctively rush away from. All that said, we promise that you can do it. What you learn in this book will work as long as you're willing to accept what you experience rather than fight it. And this new path will give you relief from the struggle, the losses, the failures. All you need to do now is keep reading . . . *and* do the work.

---

### WEEK 2
#### *Assessing the costs of my anger*

**Point to ponder:** Anger has cost me dearly. Liberating myself from the struggle with anger is a way out of the anger trap.

**Questions to consider:** Have I (and others) suffered enough from the effects of my anger behavior? Am I willing to give up trying to manage my anger feelings and go down a different path?

---

# Chapter 3

# The Heart of
# the Struggle

*You must be ready to burn yourself in your own flame:*
*how else could you become new, if you had not first become ashes?*

—Friedrich Nietzsche

## ENDING THE TUG-OF-WAR WITH ANGER

The answer to your struggle with anger may lie in the heart of the struggle itself. There's a real possibility that your struggle with anger has something to teach you, something it can reveal to you. Feeling anger is not your enemy. It's a message that something needs attending to. We will help you find out what that is and how to attend to it.

You've already taken the first step toward understanding the struggle. You've examined the costs of your anger. You've faced all your past attempts to manage and control anger thoughts, feelings, and actions. And, if you're still reading, then you've faced the difficult truth that nothing has really worked. No matter how hard you tried, no strategy to manage anger has ever helped long term. The costs are still there.

The healthiest response is to give up the struggle with anger, to surrender. By surrendering you will experience—perhaps for the first time—what your struggle with anger has really been about.

It seems like you've been fighting a tug-of-war with the anger monster pulling at one end of the rope and you pulling at the other end. Yet no matter how hard you've pulled to defeat the anger monster, it has always come back stronger, pulling harder at the other end. While you were engaged in this endless and exhausting fight, with both your hands firmly clenching the rope, it probably never occurred to you that you don't need to win this fight. What would happen if you decided to stop fighting? You could simply surrender and end the fight by dropping the rope. The anger monster would still be around, throwing the rope at you, trying to get you back into the fight. But it's your choice whether to pick up the rope again and continue the battle, or to keep your hands free so that you can start doing the things you really care about.

Dropping the rope and ending the struggle creates a doorway. If you aren't consumed with the effort to control anger, there may be an opening to see and experience something deeper, something that the struggle has masked.

# DISCOVERING THE HEART OF THE STRUGGLE

You may wonder how you can actually drop the rope. The first thing you would do is give up being a manager of anger. You can stop fighting against the feeling, the waves of upset. And when you give up being a manager of anger, you can start becoming an observer of the anger process. You can watch your thoughts, feelings, and impulses. In a moment, we'll give you some tools to help you learn to keenly observe your experience—both in the moment and retrospectively. But first, what should you watch for?

## Anger—In Five Easy Pieces

There are five components to the anger process. Each one can offer vital information about what lies at the heart of the struggle.

### Pre-Anger Feelings

The first component is your pre-anger feelings. These are emotions, as well as the physiological sensations, that precede the anger upset. Most typically, pre-anger emotions are painful, something you want to avoid. Shame and guilt are examples—both feelings attack your basic sense of self-worth. They create a feeling that you are bad or wrong at the core. Anger is a classic way to avoid these feelings. Instead of you being wrong, anger turns the tables and makes it the other person's fault.

Another pre-anger emotion is hopelessness. A lot of male depression, which has hopelessness at its root, shows up in relationships as anger. The experience of hopelessness is muted by the high-energy emotion of anger or disgust.

Other pre-anger feelings include hurt and anxiety. Both create alarm reactions. With hurt, you feel the sudden risk of abandonment; with anxiety, an imminent danger. Anger converts alarm into a drive for action and the fear goes away—at least for a while.

Bodily sensations can also play a role in your pre-anger experience. Tension in your abdomen, shoulders, or jaw can be a harbinger of upset. Feelings of heat or heaviness, agitation, headache, shakiness, and the like are frequently mentioned precursors to outbursts of anger. Anger behavior can submerge or mask all of these unpleasant sensations.

### Trigger Thoughts

The second component of the anger process is trigger thoughts. These include painful memories and images elicited by the provoking incident. Recollections of past hurts, failures, losses, and so on can become unpleasant to the point where you just desperately want to avoid them. Trigger thoughts also tend to be good/bad, right/wrong judgments about yourself or other people and their behavior. In fact, anger is virtually impossible unless your mind comes up with some type of judgment. Trigger thoughts usually paint you as a victim and blame someone else for your pain. They often contain broad labels such as stupid, incompetent, selfish, crazy, lazy, wrong, jerk, and so on.

### Anger Feeling

The third component is the anger feeling itself. It can show up as either a gradual or sudden surge of arousal. This arousal typically consists of autonomic nervous system responses, such as a pounding, rapid heartbeat, fast breathing (hyperventilation), trembling hands or legs, clenched jaw, muscle tension, and feeling hot or flushed.

### Impulse to Act

The arrival of the anger feeling usually generates a fourth component of the experience—an impulse to act. This impulse often feels indistinguishable from the trigger thoughts and anger feeling; but if you watch carefully, you can see them as distinct stages of the process. The high energy generated by escalating anger gets more unpleasant as it grows, and there's a natural pressure to discharge this anger physically. You want to do something—now—and so you begin to file through a short list of responses learned during past upsets.

### Anger Behavior

Up until this moment, you haven't actually done anything. To be sure, you have experienced quite a few changes on the inside, but nothing much has happened on the outside. Yet the pressure is mounting. Now it seems that this pressure will lead naturally to the last and most destructive component of the process, which is often some form of aggressive behavior. At the dramatic end, this includes shouting, finger pointing, flouncing away, hitting, breaking things, and the like. Sometimes anger behavior is more subtle—rolled eyes, a look of disgust, crossing your arms and looking away, a deep contemptuous sigh, cutting comments, sarcasm, gossip, emotional and physical withdrawal, and so on.

You can cycle through these five anger stages again and again during a single anger episode, and likely see this playing out multiple times over the course of a day.

### Arthur's Story

Take Arthur, for example—he and his girlfriend got into it following a complaint she made that Arthur isn't very affectionate. Arthur's pre-anger feeling was hurt with accompanying tightness in his stomach. Trigger thoughts included memories of other complaints, as well as the following self-talk: "What a hypocrite! She never hugs, never touches me, unless I start it." Then the anger feeling ignited—building fast—and included the sudden impulse to do something. In this case, it was Arthur saying something sarcastic: "That's funny, coming from someone with all the warmth of an ice tray."

The argument didn't stop there. Arthur's girlfriend came back at him: "Remember when I hugged you at your birthday party, and you wouldn't even hug me back because you didn't like the music I had on? Your arms just hung there." Now Arthur had a new pre-anger emotion—shame. It felt awful—like something was really wrong with him. He didn't want to feel that, so he started revving up for a real rage. His trigger thoughts included an image of his girlfriend turning away when he tried to kiss her later at the party, and the judgment—"I'm sick of her shit. She's totally selfish and ungiving." Now came a flush; his heart started beating like a trip-hammer. Big anger feelings equal a big need to do something. Arthur roughly pushed his girlfriend out of the way and stormed out of their apartment.

Five minutes later, his cell phone rang. "I don't need this," she said. "I won't be here when you get back." Suddenly Arthur was afraid—he felt the icy wind of abandonment. This feeling was too hard to stay with. He couldn't stand it. So the words came to him: "What a bitch!" He suddenly needed to say it out loud, and so he did. "You're a bitch," he told her, and then hung up the phone.

# BECOMING AN IMPARTIAL OBSERVER

If you want to really watch something, you have to plant yourself firmly in the present moment. The past and the future, where our thoughts so often dwell, must be abandoned in favor of the here and now. This is the place you are anyway, and where your life is lived out.

You do this, first of all, by deciding to do it. You decide you want to understand the heart of the struggle, to fully experience everything that happens when you get angry. You can make this choice any time—even right now—and commit to it.

The second way to stay in the present is by listening to your body. This is achieved by noticing your breathing, your beating heart, your posture, and your areas of tension. You observe any significant sensations in your body: areas that hurt or feel hot, heavy, or shaky. This is not an easy skill to learn, which is why we have exercises for you to practice every day, so that you can apply these skills when anger arises. If you want to apply these skills in the heat of the moment, it's best to practice them at other times first.

The third way to stay in the present is to notice and keep track of your conscious mind—your thoughts, emotions, and drives. Throughout an anger episode, you need to keep asking yourself these questions:

- What am I feeling besides anger?

- What judgments am I making—what good/bad, right/wrong thoughts are going through my mind?

- What am I driven to do right now?

The final strategy for staying in the present is to use a simple mantra to remind yourself of your role as observer: "Listen and watch; do not judge." For the observer, there is no right or wrong—there is just seeing and learning. And if you find yourself judging, then simply observe that—without judging the judging. In the end, a judgment is just another thought.

## The Advantage of Being an Observer

As an observer you can simply observe what is going on (your experience) without having to take sides or decide what is good or bad, right or wrong. Being an observer allows you to end the struggle; it's one way of dropping the rope in your tug-of-war with anger.

This is easier said than done. Anger thoughts and feelings are so strong and powerful that they can seem to rule you. In the moment you experience them, anger thoughts and feelings are difficult to distinguish from your own separate identity. It becomes difficult to see that, while thoughts, worries, and feelings are *part* of you, they aren't *you*. They come and go. You don't own them. You can't make them go away if you dislike them. You can't hold on to them, even if you like them.

A "good" thought ("I am confident") is not more like you than a "bad" thought ("I'd like to hit this guy"). They are both part of you, and they come and go all by themselves.

Think of yourself as being like a house. Just as a house provides the space for people to live in along with all their furniture and other belongings, we provide the space in which our experiences can occur. The structure of the house remains the same, regardless of who lives in it, how it's furnished, or how it's decorated. The house doesn't care about who lives in it, how people furnish it, or what they think or feel. The house simply provides the space in which all that living can occur.

## What Chess Can Teach You About Your Anger

Another way of learning to be an observer is to think about a game of chess. You have two players, a black team and a white team, with pieces that move in specified ways. Each team wants to capture the other's king. When one player makes a move, the other player can counter with a move that is offensive or defensive, strategic or reactive.

Now imagine for a moment that you're part of this game. The pieces of one team are your anger triggers (your "buttons") and the pieces of the other team are your responses. For example, when the black knight attacks ("This idiot is so lazy!"), you move your bishop to a square where he threatens the knight that attacked you ("I'll show *him!*").

Looking at your experience, ask yourself if this has ever worked with your anger. Even when you've managed to knock out one of your anger triggers, hasn't another one emerged to provoke you into action?

There's a tricky problem in this chess game because, unlike a real chess game, it is not a game with different players. In this symbolic game, the two opposing teams are really one team: you. The thoughts, feelings, and actions on both sides of the board are your thoughts, feelings, and actions. They *all* belong to you. No matter which side wins, one part of you will always be the loser.

How can you win a competition where your own thoughts and feelings compete against each other? It's like waging a war against yourself. This is a war you just can't win. So the battle goes on, every day, for years. You feel hopeless and sense that you can't win; and yet you can't stop fighting.

Let's step back for a moment and look at this situation from a different angle. What if we said that those chess pieces aren't you, anyway? Can you see what else you might be? How about the board? Let's suppose you are the board in this game. This is an important role, because without the board, there is no game. The role of the board is to provide a platform where it can all happen, and to provide the grid on which the players move.

As the board, you can see all the pieces, and you can simply watch all the action without taking sides. If you're a player, the outcome of the game is very important: you've got to beat that anger as if your life depends on it. But the board doesn't care which team seems to be winning or losing. The game just happens; who wins doesn't make any difference to the board. Being the board is a great relief, because you don't have to take sides. You're simply the place where the game is played out.

When observing your anger thoughts and feelings, you notice that some of them are painful and scary. You may not like what you think or feel and wish you felt differently. As the board, you can choose to be an impartial observer who watches the game as it progresses. You need not be a player, with a stake in the outcome of each game. Remember, your thoughts and feelings—all of them—are part of you. But they are not *you*.

The chess analogy may help you when you're having trouble separating yourself from your anger thoughts and feelings. You can tell yourself, "I am not on one team or the other. I am the board."

## MENTAL DVD

Sometimes it's impossible to track everything that's happening during an anger episode. Things move too fast and furiously. You get swept into the upset and stop noticing key thoughts and feelings. But you still want to understand what happened—to look beneath the surface of that anger and see what's hidden there. Mental DVD is a great technique for recovering forgotten details of a recent experience.

Start by closing your eyes and taking a deep breath. As you release it, try to let some of the tension drain out of your body. Now imagine a white hoop of light just above your head—like an oversized halo. The hoop of light starts to descend, surrounding first the top of your head, then moving down to your face, neck, and shoulders.

Try to relax each area of your body as the hoop passes. Take another deep breath and visualize the hoop descending to your upper arms and chest; then to your forearms and abdomen. Take another breath and watch the hoop descend to your hips, thighs, and calves, then disappear beneath your feet.

With your body more relaxed, take one last deep breath, and focus your attention on the anger episode you want to understand. Start in the middle—where you're fully angry—and imagine you're watching everything on a DVD. Observe the scene for a minute. You're really steamed. On this disk, there's a voice-over of your thoughts—listen to what's going on in your mind.

Now hit the button that takes you back to the beginning of the episode, before the anger started. Press Play. Watch the action; listen to what's being said. What are you feeling in that moment before the anger? Are you hurt, ashamed, scared, hopeless, guilty, feeling wrong or unworthy? Pay attention to your posture and your voice. Try to make contact with what's happening inside you just before the anger surges.

Now notice any memories or images that have been triggered. What are your thoughts? Do you have trigger thoughts that paint the other person or the situation as bad or wrong? Keep listening until you hear the words of this inner monologue.

Now the anger is coming. Watch as it grows. Notice what it feels like, what it makes you want to do. Be aware of any impulses to speak or act on your anger. Don't do anything about your feelings. Just be the house or the chessboard (as in the sections above), and let your feelings be. Just observe them.

# MAPPING YOUR ANGER PROCESS

Now that you have some tools to help you observe your anger, it's time to map how your anger really works—the process of your anger. For the next week, closely watch each anger episode. Use the techniques we've suggested to remain a here-and-now observer of your experience.

Adopt the house or chessboard perspective, and watch what's going on. Or use the mental DVD to recapture an anger event that was too overwhelming to track as it unfolded. What have you learned? Record as much detail as you can in the following anger map exercise. Use a separate piece of paper for your answers if you need more room.

## YOUR ANGER MAP

### Pre-Anger Feelings

Describe the emotions and physical sensations you noticed this week preceding your anger. Is there typically one feeling, or are there several that may show up at the beginning of your anger process? How do these feelings affect your sense of self-worth? Do you find yourself wanting to escape or suppress them? Are there physical sensations preceding anger that are painful or uncomfortable? Does anger help to push them out of your awareness?

_____

_____

_____

_____

### Trigger Thoughts

Write down as much as you can remember about any painful images or memories that come up in anger situations. What judgments do you typically make about other people? Which of your expectations or rules for living do they fail to live up to? Note how your trigger thoughts may change your pre-anger feeling or distract you from them.

_____

_____

_____

_____

## Anger Feeling

Does your anger build slowly, or suddenly ignite full force? Does it sometimes stick around and fester for long periods of time, like a low-grade cold? Does it feel good, sweeping away hurt or shame? Does it feel scary or disturbing? Write everything you've learned as an observer of your anger, every detail about the feeling and its effect on you. Note particularly what happened to your pre-anger feelings and any changes in your trigger thoughts.

_____

_____

_____

_____

## Impulse to Act

What did you want to do this week when your anger surged? What images or thoughts came to mind? Write down everything you imagined saying or doing. You may have done only some or perhaps none of those things, but it's important to identify as many anger-driven impulses as possible. How did you decide whether or not to act on them?

_____

_____

_____

_____

## Anger Behavior

Write down what you actually did, via gestures, facial expressions, words, tone of voice, or overt behavior (acts of aggression, violence) as a response to your anger. How did the aggression feel at the moment? How did it affect your anger (both the emotion and physical sensations)? As time went on, how did your feelings change, if at all, regarding your anger behavior?

_____

_____

_____

_____

## EXAMPLE ANGER MAP

Here's how Julia, a thirty-eight-year-old nurse in a convalescent hospital, completed the anger map exercise.

### Pre-Anger Feelings

*Embarrassment when I'm criticized. Feeling I'm not good enough, that I'm a messed-up person. It's the same feeling with my husband, with the head nurse, with my kid when he's on my case for something. It's a horrible feeling—like I'm a piece of crap on someone's shoe and I just want to stop it. I notice that I want to throw something between me and the feeling—so it can't stab at me. The physical stuff is like this sick, sinking feeling and this "all is lost" feeling. It's in my stomach, and it goes along with feeling I've done something wrong.*

### Trigger Thoughts

*Images of past embarrassing mistakes. Then my first thought is, "No, shut up, don't say that." And then I notice myself thinking, "They shouldn't be doing this to me; they don't know what they're talking about." Sometimes that turns into something wrong with them, some flaw or another that I can pick on. And I just focus on that, and try to remember examples of it—situations where they've really screwed up. I expect people to be kind and supportive, and when they're not, I really hate that. Really judge it. The trigger thoughts seem to put space between me and the embarrassment, the feeling*

I've done something wrong. It's like I'm distracted by them; thinking those thoughts instead of feeling bad.

## Anger Feeling

It comes over me in a few seconds. I'm hot, my heart starts pounding. I'm totally zeroed in on the person I'm pissed at. And suddenly that's all there is—the anger. It's so big, I'm instantly overwhelmed. I'm scared that I'm going to explode (whatever that means). There's an incredibly tight feeling in my gut. And it's like I'm speeding, in this big rush that's overpowering me. It's kind of too much. But I don't know how to stop it. All the other feelings are gone now, blasted out of existence by the anger. I have no awareness that I ever felt ashamed. It's just, these . . . holes. Gotta get away from these holes.

## Impulse to Act

I want to shout, scare them, make them go away. I want to shout, "My husband is a hypocrite." And sometimes I have an image of slapping him. And I definitely want to slap my son and scream that he needs to be more respectful. A million things flash through my mind with my head nurse. I want to shout, "Why don't you try my job instead of sitting at that desk all day? When's the last time you did bed pans, when's the last time you got crap on your uniform?" And while I'm imagining all these things I could say, I'm scared at the same time for what would happen, how I'd screw up the relationships. There's a voice in my head saying: "You better not."

## Anger Behavior

I flounce away from my husband and won't talk to him. I go totally cold. I do yell at my son. I called him "a punk, with no f—ing gratitude" yesterday. With my boss, I go, "Fine, fine, whatever you say," in this really cold voice. I notice now, whatever I do, it doesn't make my anger better. I go on feeling upset and horrible. I think yelling or getting real icy will help it, but my heart just keeps on pounding and I have to just wait till it subsides.

# THE BIG QUESTION: ARE YOU READY FOR A CHANGE?

The path out of your anger and into your life will take you to places you've never been before. Some of these places may be scary and difficult for you to experience, at least early on. Yet there is something at the core of this struggle that is soft and has extraordinary value: protecting a delicate human being (you) who fears two things—that people will judge and reject you and that you will reject and hate yourself.

The fear is that you will finally be seen—by yourself or others—as unworthy, broken, or bad. The only hope is to stay hidden. Safe. Protected from those pre-anger feelings by trigger thoughts and rage. That vulnerable self you've been shielding has always felt like it could be broken or mutilated if the arrows of judgment were ever allowed to hit home. So you remain vigilant, on guard, and angry.

Anger is a way of protecting that delicate human being. It masks the feelings of inadequacy, hurt, shame, and guilt and keeps them out of view. Think, for a moment, what it feels like to have your buttons pushed. When others, either by their words or by their actions, push your buttons, you become angry, in part because those buttons represent aspects of yourself (including your past) that are painful, hurtful, and embarrassing to acknowledge openly and directly. A lot of us feel this way. When our buttons are pushed, the totality of who we are is right in our face, and not entirely by our own doing. Anger is a natural reaction to this process. We feel wronged and then we act on it to defend that fragile self that has been brought out in the open; this way we can push those unwanted feelings and old hurts and pains back out of view.

Here's a novel idea: What if all this protecting and defending and hiding is the problem? What if there is no need to hide anything? What if letting go of those painful feelings, of those moments of hurt and judgment, of the fear of being seen and rejected is the beginning of an answer?

You've tried the old way—running away from the pain—long enough. It hasn't worked. It only creates more problems; the struggle just keeps playing out in your life. Are you ready for a change? What if you were to stop struggling and drop the rope? What if you started to be an observer rather than a member of one team or the other?

Simply noticing what you feel means beginning to accept what you feel. It does not mean liking what you feel or agreeing with what somebody has done to you. It only means being aware of what you feel and acknowledging it for what it is (a thought, a feeling, a sensation, a memory, an image), without taking sides or doing anything about it.

In the coming chapters, we'll provide you with several exercises that will help you become an expert observer.

## THE TAKE-HOME MESSAGE

Protecting your vulnerable self from hurt and pain using anger and blame is at the core of your futile struggle with anger. This has not worked; instead, it has caused numerous problems in your life. As you learn to acknowledge anger thoughts and feelings for what they really are, it will become easier to give up your struggle with anger. Learning to become an observer is a skill that can bring remarkable relief from suffering.

---

### WEEK 3
#### Discovering the heart of my struggle with anger

**Points to ponder:** I can learn to become an observer of, rather than a participant in, my anger. I am not my thoughts and feelings.

**Questions to consider:** Do I really need to hide and protect myself from feeling hurt, shame, fear, and inadequacy? Am I willing to learn to be an observer of anger feelings and thoughts rather than participating in a struggle with them?

# Chapter 4

# Controlling Anger and Hurt Is the Problem

*Holding on to anger is like grasping a hot coal with the intent of throwing it at someone else; you are the one who gets burned.*

—Gautama Siddhārta

If you're reading this book, chances are that a good deal of your life has been colored by anger, rage, unresolved hurt, and pain. This may be hard for you to face squarely. You may still believe that managing and controlling anger is a way out. Yet you've been down that path, and it hasn't solved your anger problem. Each so-called solution—each attempt to stop or slow down the pain, to manage and control it—has gotten you to this place. And you're still angry.

We know that most seemingly sensible solutions to anger problems are really about control. The voice in your head tells you to control anger. This voice comes from the belief that anger is dangerous; that it's impossible to feel anger and still live a good life.

The voice is lying to you. Controlling anger doesn't work in the same way that control works in other areas of life. In this chapter you'll learn why. You'll also learn how to begin letting go of the anger control agenda and get on with your life.

# TWO PLACES WHERE CONTROL DOESN'T WORK

Trying to control areas of your life where you don't have much control is a surefire guarantee of disappointment and anger. There are some situations where desirable choices seem nonexistent—severe illness, deception by a partner, or getting laid off from a job (to name a few). People can usually see that such situations are out of their control, and they don't beat themselves up for not being able to make things turn out differently.

Most angry people feel they must struggle mightily to get a grip on their angry thoughts and feelings. Struggling with what you think and feel may be how you have learned to cope with your anger. You may even beat yourself up for not being able to control your hurt, pain, and disappointment. You're not alone; it's natural to think that you *should* be able to control them.

But the problem with control strategies is this: they work just enough to keep your painful feelings at bay, but in the long run you're left feeling angry and hurt. Once this cycle of struggle and control is set into motion, it can take over and become the dominant feature of your life.

The good news is that there are still some constructive choices available. But you have to learn to distinguish what you can control from what you can't. To reach this goal, you'll need to face how your struggle for control has failed you with your anger. We'll help you look deeply into this struggle so that you come to see it for what it is.

Everyone's anger stems from two main sources: their struggle to control other people and their struggle to control painful emotions such as anger and shame.

## You Can't Control Other People

Angry people go to great lengths to exert control over other people. You may achieve an illusion of control with infants and very young children, but it's impossible to even fool yourself when it comes to exerting control over older children and adults. The goal of control will fail 99 percent of the time.

When you try to control others, you're operating under the mistaken assumption that other people in your life ought to behave, think, and act like you think they should. The plain and simple truth is that other people don't like feeling controlled, and neither do you. Trying to control others sends the message that you do not accept them for who they are. You are expressing mistrust of their judgment— in effect, putting them beneath you.

Here your mind machine is feeding you two lies. First, it is telling you that you have the right to control others. The second lie is that you actually have the ability to control others. Both are fundamentally false. You can't force your way into the minds of other people, just as other people can't force their way into your head to dictate how you feel, think, or behave. If you think you can do this, then you're only kidding yourself. When you act to control others, we can give you a 100 percent guarantee that they will eventually find ways to resist and run from you. We can also promise you that your efforts will leave you feeling frustrated and angry.

### Control over Others Is Illusory: A Self-Inventory

Below is a list of behaviors driven by efforts to control other people. All these efforts eventually fuel anger, frustration, conflict, bitterness, and alienation. Take stock of your behavior as you go through the list and check off each statement that applies to you:

☐ I routinely offer advice that is unwanted by pleading, persuading, or lecturing.

☐ I repeat a point over and over in an effort to get others to align their thoughts and views with mine.

☐ I communicate by telling rather than discussing.

☐ I use "shoulds," "musts," "had betters," and similar absolute statements when communicating.

☐ I use my anger to get my message across or force compliance in others.

☐ I use dogmatic statements, stubborn noncompliance, closed-mindedness, or chilling silence to influence others.

☐ I impose my choices, beliefs, and standards on others with unyielding stubbornness of conviction.

☐ I discount the behaviors, values, thoughts, opinions, and choices of others as wrongheaded and in need of my correction.

☐ I procrastinate or give a halfhearted effort as a way to get back or get even.

☐ I tend to be impatient with myself and other people.

☐ I feel uneasy about loose ends and strive for closure, even if it hurts me or others.

The following exercise will help you see the problems that arise when you try to control other people. All you need to do here is imagine that you are a puppeteer. The show you are about to put on is entitled *Magical Mind Control over People Who Make Me Feel Pissed Off.*

## THE HUMAN PUPPETEER IN MAGICAL MIND CONTROL

Take a moment to think of the characters involved in a recent anger episode where you were trying to get others to do as you willed. Then, go to your imaginary puppet box and pull out the marionettes, one for each character in the show. From your perch high above the stage, you begin to play out the anger scene below you. Try to play it out as you would have wanted it to go. As you do, notice how easy it is to get all the characters to do as you wish. You can make them bend over, gesture, and do whatever you want them to do. If you think "That person is making a stupid request," you can simply replace what that person says with whatever you wish them to say in that moment. You can get them to think and say what you'd like to hear, and to show emotions that you think are appropriate in the situation. You and only you have control over the puppets.

Now, let's mix this up a bit. In the sequel, real people dressed to look like marionettes are the characters in this show. As before, you are high above the stage in your perch. The actors are still connected to the strings. But as you try to replay the scene, you notice that the characters are not doing what you are trying to will them to do. You want them to go left, but they go right. You say "They shouldn't be doing that," and you pull the strings, but now you feel them pulling back, resisting you. You try to force them to think and say this or that but hear them saying something else. You become frustrated because you really don't know what they're thinking and feeling and you have no way to get them to do what you wish. You feel anger building—the human puppets are running this show, not you!

The real-life marionettes in this sequel are playing out the scene just as they should, because they are human beings. Unlike the puppets, they control their choices and actions, what they say and do on this stage. You, meanwhile, are powerless over them. But you are *not* powerless over how you respond to them. You have control over what you do here. You can either fight the characters and engage in a struggle, or you can let go of the strings and simply allow the characters to do as they would do, think as they would think, feel as they would feel, without trying to change how they play out their roles. You can simply watch, trusting that the characters know what is best for them, that they may choose to do this or that, and that in the end, they— not you—are holding their own strings. You hold your strings.

## You Can't Control Your Emotional Reactions

Recognizing that you hold your own strings in life will put you face-to-face with your own pain, hurt, and other emotions, both positive and negative. You may think, "Well, if I can't control other people, then maybe I can control the negative energy and thoughts that arise in my mind and body when I hurt and feel angry." This sensible-sounding solution is unfortunately another dead end. Control over your emotional reactions is just as illusory as your desire to control other people.

### Anger Is Not a Real Hot Stove

Life has taught you how well control works to help you avoid physical sources of pain and harm in your life. When you were very young, someone probably told you not to touch the hot stove [or the iron or the heater] because you could get hurt. Keeping your hand away from touching whatever was hot kept you safe and prevented injury. This very sensible and reasonable strategy has repeated itself over and over again in both obvious and subtle ways in your life, because it generally works to keep you alive and unharmed.

But using this same strategy to manage or run from painful experiences that are happening inside you hasn't worked nearly as well. When unpleasant thoughts show up and you try to stuff them, guess what you get? More unpleasant thoughts. When emotional hurt and pain show up and you try to avoid them, guess what you get? Some temporary relief, but at a cost of more pain and suffering later on. The problem here is that the same programming that helps you stay alive and safe when real danger shows up doesn't work when you apply it to unpleasant thoughts and feelings happening inside you.

## Martha's Story

Martha was a longtime master of suppressing her anger and hurt. On the outside, she was a calm and cool operator, wife and mother of three children, and an active member of her church. She had stressors: running the home and taking care of most of the housework, caring for her ailing parents who lived nearby, shuttling the kids to and from a full schedule of after-school activities, all the while trying to maintain a viable home business. Few could tell that these stressors weighed heavily on her. She had developed a routine of low friction. There was little conflict in her family, and Martha always maintained a calm demeanor, greeting everyone with a big smile.

All of this came to a head when her husband expressed interest in taking a weeklong fishing trip with his friends. That's when Martha exploded in a rage of tears, "Go ahead—take a trip! You always put yourself first anyway!" Her husband reacted defensively, for he too had a very busy work schedule and hadn't gotten away by himself for many years. This was a legitimate need. Martha likewise had legitimate needs: time with her husband, a break to recharge and unwind, and support and help managing the family and her other obligations. The confrontation quickly escalated. Both aired old hurts and ugly feelings, and they flung accusations back and forth about things that happened long ago. Finally, Martha said, "I can't take this bullshit anymore" and stormed out of the room. Then she took the kids with her to stay with her parents.

This ugly exchange was the result of years of suppressed anger and emotional pain. Small issues were never addressed openly. Feelings were never discussed or acknowledged. Emotional and psychological batteries were slowly and steadily depleted and never recharged. From the outside, Martha, her husband, and her family seemed free from anger and conflict—they fit the Ozzie and Harriet image. Yet, things had been piling up over time and eating at everyone little by little. So one day a seemingly small incident broke the proverbial camel's back, with disastrous consequences. This is what happens when you try to suppress anger.

Suppression is about ignoring legitimate needs and failing to accept what is going on inside you. It follows from an unwillingness to address concerns openly, for fear that openness will be useless and uncomfortable. Mind traps fuel it. You know the self-talk, the voice in your head that tells you that living the good life means that you must shut out all hurt, pain, and unpleasant emotions and memories. The result is that you deny your humanity and may find yourself hurting and upset inside. Meanwhile the energy grows and, like a powder keg, the energy explodes in anger. This is what happens when you fight a battle with your unpleasant feelings and thoughts.

You've been down this road. You've probably treated your anger much like you would when faced with a red-hot stove. You try to pull away because anger, like the hot stove, seems dangerous. So when anger shows up, you must do something about it. Yet, pulling away from a hot stove or other potential sources of real pain and harm rarely works in the same way when applied to your painful thoughts and emotions.

## Why You Can't Control Anger and Emotional Pain

Numerous studies (for example, Purdon 1999 and Wegner 1994) have shown that when people act to get rid of emotional and psychological pain, they end up instead with more emotional and psychological pain. All of what we know about dealing with human emotional pain boils down to this simple fact. You can't keep your unpleasant thoughts and emotions from burning you in the way you can pull your hand away from a hot stove. There's no on and off switch you can use to highlight or deep-six your thoughts and emotions.

In fact, trying to control unpleasant emotions, internal bodily sensations, and even disturbing thoughts will mostly backfire. You'll get more of the very thing you don't want to think and feel. This happens because your body is a system with a built-in system of feedback loops—your brain and nervous system. When you act against parts of this system—suppressing, avoiding, stuffing painful feelings—it sends out reverberations to all other parts of the system. This mind-body connection is like a sensitive spiderweb in this respect. Everything is connected.

Suppression and control take enormous effort. As in a spiderweb, the effort required to keep one part of the system in check sends small vibrations out to all other parts of the web. The vibrations eventually return to whatever it is you are trying to keep at bay. Suppressing unpleasant experiences—be they thoughts, memories, anger, anxiety, hurt, or bodily sensations—actually makes matters worse. Why?

Maybe we can draw a parallel with trying not to think about a pink elephant. Go ahead and try! This is pretty much impossible, because the thought "Don't think about the pink elephant" is itself, obviously, a thought about a pink elephant. The more you try not to have this thought, the more of this thought you'll have. The same is true of unpleasant thoughts, feelings, and some internal bodily sensations. The take-home message here is this: You can't win a fight against yourself.

Such struggles with yourself are fueled largely by an unwillingness to make space for every aspect of your experience and identity. Your mind would like you to believe that to be happy and to live life fully, you must get rid of your painful and unpleasant thoughts, feelings, or memories. To have the "good life" means that you must be pain free. So you struggle to manage, stuff, bury, deny, or medicate the hurt and pain. All this time spent controlling tends to get in the way of what most people wish to spend their time doing—the experiences and relationships that you'd probably much rather be having.

The simple lesson here is this: Control works against you when applied to unwanted and painful aspects of your private world, just as it works against you when you try to impose it on other people. In both cases, you are sending a message that diminishes your own and others' humanity and dignity. This is no way to live.

To get out of this cycle, you'll need to first come to terms with the fact that deliberate control is not a solution. It is the problem. Your thoughts and feelings—the good, the bad, and the ugly—always go with you wherever you go. These experiences define what is uniquely human about you. You cannot escape or avoid them so long as you're alive. They are part of you. To act against them is to act against your very being. To act against them means that you will remain stuck in hurt and anger.

### Suppression and Control Are About Pain Avoidance: A Self-Inventory

All efforts to suppress and control anger are fundamentally about pain avoidance. The goal is to make the hurt go away. This goal is unattainable; it's a dead end. Covering up hurt with anger does not make hurt go away. Instead it bottles the energy. As in Martha's case, it stores it for release at a later time. The release later on might take the form of unfettered anger. Or it may show up as depression, anxiety, panic attacks, or physical symptoms such as headaches, ulcers, backaches, and fatigue. We don't have to convince you that none of these are good for you.

Let's have a look at how you may be suppressing your emotional pain and hurt. Below is a partial list of behaviors that suggest you're in the habit of suppressing your anger. Read each statement carefully, and think about them as they apply to your life. Take stock of your behavior as you go through the list, and put a check mark in front of each statement that applies to you.

☐ I tend to hide my painful feelings for fear that nothing good can come from emotional transparency.

☐ I act to push out of my mind upsetting thoughts or memories.

☐ I avoid feeling unpleasant emotions and act to reduce them quickly.

☐ I habitually stuff my feelings or use distraction, alcohol, or other drugs and strategies to feel better.

☐   I resort to anger to mask other unpleasant emotions and thoughts.

☐   I see my emotional hurt and pain as real barriers to living the life I want and becoming the person I want to be.

☐   I tend to withdraw from problems, even if that means they are left unresolved.

☐   I refuse to air personal problems, needs, or concerns.

☐   I focus on maintaining the appearance of having it all together.

☐   I avoid controversial or troublesome topics.

☐   I second-guess my own choices.

☐   I play the role of people pleaser by putting myself second.

☐   I let my hurt and frustration pass without discussing it.

☐   I pretend that I don't have resentment, or that all is rosy in my life.

The following exercise will help you more fully experience the futility of trying to control your anger and emotional pain. It will also show you why struggling with unpleasant feelings and thoughts makes them worse.

## YOU'RE WIRED TO A PERFECT POLYGRAPH, AND ZAP!

To begin, find a quiet place where you can sit and get comfortable. Imagine that you're connected to the best and most sensitive polygraph machine that's ever been built. Because this polygraph is incredibly effective in detecting anger, there is no way you can be aroused or angry without the machine detecting it. Now here is your task (it sounds quite simple): All you have to do is stay relaxed—just stay calm—while thinking about a recent episode where you felt really pissed off. If you get the least bit angry or aroused, however, this machine will detect it.

We know how important it is to you to be successful here, so we're going to give you a special incentive to succeed. If you can stay completely relaxed while you imagine the anger scene, then we'll give you $100,000! (Funny money here, but try to imagine that you would really get that cash payout.) The catch is that the polygraph is designed to give you a deadly shock if you show the slightest bit of anger or arousal. So long as you stay relaxed, you won't die. But if you get the least bit angry or aroused—and remember, this perfect polygraph will notice that immediately—the machine will deliver the shock and kill you. So, just relax!

Take a moment to consider how impossible it would be to survive in this situation. You might react by saying to yourself, "Oh my God! I'm getting tense and angry! Here it comes—zap!" The tiniest bit of anger or arousal would be terrifying for you or for any other person in this situation.

There is no way to stay calm when you are already connected to the perfect polygraph: your nervous system, which is better than any lie detector at searching out anger or arousal. If you've been struggling to squelch your anger feelings, the very workability of your life may seem to be at stake. When anger and emotional pain show up, you struggle to keep them at bay. But you only get angrier and feel more pain. Your nervous system kicks in and guess what you get? You get zapped!

# CHOICES, ACTIONS, DESTINY: THREE AREAS WHERE YOU DO HAVE CONTROL

Conscious, deliberate, purposeful control works well in the external world outside your skin wherever the following rule applies: "If you don't like what you are doing, figure out a way to change it or get rid of it using your hands and feet. Then go ahead and do it."

Unfortunately, this rule does not apply to internal events that occur inside your skin, such as anger feelings, painful thoughts, and other emotions. Rather than trying to change these, you are far better off refocusing your attention and expending your energy on the three areas where you *do* have control: your choices, your actions, and your destiny.

## Only You Have Control over the Choices You Make

You have full response-ability for the choices you make. Coming to terms with this can feel both sobering and liberating. For instance, you cannot choose whether you feel hurt or angry. Yet you can decide what you do with that hurt and anger. You can choose to ruminate on your hurt and anger, run from it, or bury and hide it. You also have the option of doing nothing about the feelings and thoughts. You can decide to let them be or actively meet them with compassion and patience.

As you learn to recognize that every moment of your life is about choices, you free yourself from being a slave to your impulses, your resentments, and your anger. In essence, you're free to choose how you respond to triggers for anger and what you do with your emotional pain and anger when you feel it. It's your choice whether you behave in a kind, forgiving, or accepting fashion while recognizing your painful feelings; or whether you give in to your impulse to either deny your anger or act on it.

### Taking Stock of Where You Have Response Choices

Let's take a look at some specific places where you have the power to choose:

- Meeting your hurt and anger with compassion and forgiveness versus struggling with it to stuff or deny it

- Hearing what others have to say (even if you disagree with them) versus refusing to listen and giving them advice they don't want

- Speaking words of acceptance and understanding versus words of judgment and blame

- Letting go of old hurts, resentments, and painful memories versus holding on to them

- Practicing patience with others and yourself versus blowing up in anger and frustration

- Acting in ways that uphold your humanity and dignity as well as that of others *or* acting in ways that shame and demean

- Moving forward in your life with anger *or* struggling with it and remaining stuck

## BRAINSTORMING ALTERNATIVES
## TO ANGER BEHAVIOR

For this exercise, you'll need to recall an upsetting situation that brought on feelings of anger, blame, rage, and other unpleasant thoughts and feelings. (We provide some examples below.) Once you have the scene clearly in mind, go ahead and list the main triggers (whether people, thoughts, or feelings), bodily sensations and emotions that you felt, and, lastly, how you coped or behaved in this situation. Be as specific as you can. This exercise has similarities to the anger management history you completed in chapter 2, but this exercise will take you further.

Here's how Andy, an eighteen-year-old grocery clerk, completed the first part:

**People trigger:** *My father criticized me.*

**Feeling trigger:** *Feeling frustrated and hurt.*

**Emotions and bodily sensations:** *Irritable. Anxious. Heart is racing and pounding in my chest. Surge of adrenaline. Tense in neck and shoulders. Feeling sad and humiliated.*

**My anger behavior (how I coped):** *Acted tough. Told him to "shut the fuck up." Called him "a bitter old man and a lazy son of a bitch." I left and drove to my friend's house and vowed to keep away from my dad. Spent time venting with friends about how much of a dick he is. Smoked a few cigarettes. Tried to think about reasons why my dad has to be such a jerk.*

Now comes the more difficult part: brainstorming alternative choices to anger behavior. Start with the triggers and see how they ultimately led to self-destructive anger behavior. Rewind the tape, and for each trigger, see if you can brainstorm other choices, apart from anger behavior, you had available to you in that moment. For a hint, take a look at your coping strategy. You'll want to come up with fundamentally different choices than the ones you listed under coping strategies and anger behavior. As you do, be mindful that there are no right or wrong answers here. These are your choices—what you do and can do for yourself. Later on, we'll guide you through this process more deeply. With practice, you'll find that you do have a broad range of choices when anger and hurt show up. Acting on anger is one choice among many other choices.

After Andy fleshed out this scene, he then went back and brainstormed other choices he had available to him. Here's how he completed the brainstorming part of the exercise:

**People triggers:** *I had absolutely no control over what my dad decided to say. My dad's choice of words and his actions are not my responsibility. He can say or do as he wishes. I can choose to simply listen. I've heard this stuff before. I don't have to let my triggers be engaged. I can just let the words be without reacting to them.*

**Feeling triggers:** *The frustration and hurt I feel are my own. I can simply notice what my body is doing here. I can decide not to push the feeling away, but not to use it as fuel for anger. I can just let it be, and experience it for what it is.*

**Emotions and bodily sensations:** *There is really nothing I can do about what my body is doing right now. What I'm feeling is unpleasant, but I don't need to run from it. I can choose to sit still with the energy and do nothing to make it go away. I can allow the energy go away on its own.*

**My anger behavior (how I respond):** *I can see that I have lots of choices here. I can choose to listen to my dad or leave. I can choose to respond to him in a calm voice by letting him know that I feel hurt and sad when he says those things to me, even though I'm boiling over inside; or I can confront him with a loud voice, name-calling, screaming, and leaving. I can extend compassion to my dad and let him know that I do love him, even though his words drive me crazy. Or, I can act in ways that do not reflect my love for him as another human being. I can decide not to run from my dad, because this relationship is important to me. I can choose to carry the hurt and pain with me to my friend's house, or let it go. I can choose to gossip and vent with my friends about my dad, or I can choose not to do that. Venting really did nothing to resolve the situation with my dad. I could have taken a walk instead of reaching for a cigarette. I also could have decided to do something less damaging to my health, like listening to some music.*

Above all, Andy began to appreciate that how he responded to this situation was his own responsibility. Only he could do things to meet his needs and uphold his values. The same is true of you. The choices you make can lead you to anger and misery or the life you want to create and nurture.

## You Can Control Your Actions

Your actions, in this chapter, are anything you do with your hands, feet, and mouth—how you respond to the thoughts, memories, physical sensations, and feelings dished out by your body and mind.

Let's say you feel hurt. Then you act on it; perhaps you lash out with blame and accusations, or you shut down by withdrawing. These are both actions. Alternatively, you might do nothing about the hurt and simply notice it for what it is (not for what your mind says it is). You focus on doing things in your life that matter to you, even if that means taking the hurt along for the ride. Either way, you're doing something. But your choice of actions, in a very real sense, helps define who you are and what your life will be about.

Control works extremely well when you apply it to your actions. For instance, if you want to clean up your yard, you can go and get a rake and get started. If you want to perform an act of kindness, you can do something nice for someone. If you want to change the color of the walls in a room in your home, you can paint them. You may decide to reconnect with an old friend by picking up the phone and calling or sending an e-mail. You can exercise regularly and watch what you eat and drink to promote your health and well-being. You can take an aspirin for a headache, see a doctor for an illness or injury, and take time out to relax. The common element in these life examples is this: They all involve actions—what you do with your hands, feet, and, at times, your mouth. Other people can see what you do and hear what you say. This is a critical point in terms of your anger.

You know how difficult it is to control the feeling of anger. You may also have difficultly controlling anger behavior. Impulses to act are strong, and it's easy to feel overwhelmed by them. But even an impulse to act is still a feeling. There is a split second between the impulse and the action when you can intervene, determining what you're going to do and how you're going to respond. You can step back and ask yourself, "Is it really necessary to act on this emotion [or this thought]?" You have control in this moment, no matter how powerful the anger feelings, hurt, and impulses to act.

Ask yourself what has cost you more, your anger feelings or your anger behavior. If you were born on this planet, your anger behavior has cost you far more than your anger feelings. Nobody else knows what you truly think and feel inside. Your anger only manifests itself to others through what you do with your hands, feet, and mouth. You've paid for your actions, not your thoughts or feelings. Your actions are what have gotten you into trouble. This is where you need to take charge and make changes.

## You Can Control Your Destiny

Controlling your destiny is the real prize. The cumulative effect of your choices and your actions will determine what your life will become—in other words, your destiny. This does not mean that the out-

*Figure 1.* "Emotional Avoidance Detour" was conceptualized and illustrated by Dr. Joseph Ciarrochi and Dr. David Mercer, University of Wollongong, New South Wales, Australia. Reprinted with permission of the authors.

come of your choices and your actions will always be what you desire; remember, you can't control what others do, think, and feel. And there are many events in life, both good and bad, that occur outside your control. What most people hope for is that the cumulative effect of their choices and actions will yield a sense that their life was well lived. Everything you do from here on out adds up to that. Choice is destiny.

## CHOICES AND ACTIONS—
## MY LIFE AND MY DESTINY

Imagine you are driving through life on a long road toward a mountain. Let's call this mountain your "Value Mountain." It represents everything you care about in your life, and what you want to be about as a person. This is the place you want to go. You are driving happily along the road toward your Value Mountain, and suddenly anger jumps out and blocks the road. You slow down and try to avoid hitting anger. You quickly turn right, and find yourself on the "control and emotional avoidance" detour. But this detour simply goes round and round in a circle. You stay there because the anger, pain, hurt, and shame are still blocking the road. So you go round and round, waiting, hoping, but getting nowhere. You feel bad about getting nowhere. You feel mad at the anger and shame for blocking the road. You watch as your life seems to be ticking by.

This is what happens when people engage in a struggle with their unpleasant thoughts and feelings. They feel stuck, going round and round in circles and getting nowhere. Nobody wants their life to be about driving on the control-and-avoidance detour. And yet it's so easy to get caught in this detour when anger and pain show up.

But there's an alternative. You can take the anger, pain, unpleasant thoughts, and physical sensations with you on your ride through life without acting on them. You can choose to drive forward with them—in part because choosing the alternative costs you. The first and most important task here is to make a choice to do something fundamentally different about your hurt, pain, and anger. The second part requires that you be willing to take what you're thinking and feeling with you as you engage in actions that move you forward. Unless you do, you'll continue to feel stuck and trapped by your anger.

## Recognizing the Struggle for Control and Letting It Go

Letting go of the struggle for control is not as hard as it may seem. It begins with you making a decision to do so. The hardest part is putting your decision into action. One of the chief barriers to action is failing to recognize the difference between what you can control and what you cannot control. Falling back into the old control agenda where control is not possible is a surefire way to stay stuck and to allow anger to sidetrack you from what you want your life to be about.

To get unstuck and stay that way, you'll need to develop greater ease in the early detection of situations where control is possible in your life; those are the places where you need to spend your time and effort working. The exercise below is designed to help you to do just that. You can think of it as a sort of review and preparation for the hard work to come.

## DISCRIMINATING BETWEEN WHAT I CAN AND CANNOT CONTROL

Read each statement and then, without much thought, circle the number next to each situation you believe can be controlled by you. Don't circle the numbers where you think the situation is outside your control.

1. What someone else is thinking

2. The choices I make

3. Others being on time

4. How I respond to other people

5. What other people value and care about

6. What I say in a situation

7. The thoughts I may have from time to time

8. The direction I want my life to take

9. How others respond to me (my choices, actions, and expressed thoughts and feelings)

10. How I behave with respect to other people

11. The choices others make

12. How I speak with other people

13. The behavior of pets (mine and others')

14. How I respond to my thoughts and feelings (positive, negative, neutral)

15. Whether other people follow rules or standards

16. Whether I am on time and follow through with commitments

17. What others do

18. Whether I follow certain rules or standards

19. Whether other people like me

20. Whether I prepare for tasks and do my best

21. What I feel at any point

22. What I do with my precious time on this earth

23. Experiences in life that do not involve me directly (weather, equipment failures, political decisions)

24. My values and what I care about

Now go back and look at the numbers you circled. All the odd-numbered statements represent situations where you have absolutely no control. You may imagine otherwise; but if you go back and think carefully, you will see that you truly do not have control in any of these scenarios.

Your mind may say you do or "should have" control of some of these odd-numbered situations. This is part of the problem. Remember, when you struggle to control what you cannot control, you will only end up feeling hurt, angry, and disappointed. Anger needs this struggle to grow. When these situations show up, you need to recognize them for what they are, stop, and then look for places where you can exert control over your choices and actions with an eye on what you want your life to be about.

The even-numbered situations represent a sampling of life circumstances where you do have control. They share one thing in common: they represent your actions, what you say or do.

## THE TAKE-HOME MESSAGE

The path out of anger is learning to recognize the difference between what you can and can't control. This entire book is about learning to live out this important distinction. You cannot control your emotional reactions or what other people do. You can control your choices and actions, what you say, and what you do, including how you respond to your anger, to your pain, and to other people. You can control your efforts and contributions toward life and the welfare of others, both at home and at work. You can choose how you respond to your thoughts, memories, feelings, physical sensations, and choices you've made. You can control how you respond to other people—without trying to control them. The challenge for you will be to drop the rope in your tug-of-war with anger in situations where control won't work, while learning to focus on areas of your life where you do have control. All the remaining chapters are about fostering your ability to choose, take action, and move forward in your life. They are about maximizing control where you have it.

---

### WEEK 4
#### Trying to control the uncontrollable
#### is the problem

**Point to ponder:** Control is often illusory. The trick is to recognize what you can control—your choices, your actions, your destiny.

**Questions to consider:** Where do I needlessly try to apply control in my life? What have my vain attempts at control cost me? Am I willing to give up trying to control what I cannot control so I can move forward with my life?

---

# Chapter 5

# How Your Mind Creates Anger

*Thinking that gets us into trouble: "Other people must treat me considerately and kindly and in the way I want them to treat me. If they don't, they deserve to be blamed, damned, and punished for their inconsideration."*

—Albert Ellis

We are hardwired to evaluate everything that happens to and around us. Our minds must decide if an experience is dangerous or safe, harmful or benign. We've survived as a species by identifying things that threaten us and avoiding them. So far, so good. These built-in responses help keep us alive. They lead us away from pain and danger, while pushing us toward nourishment and safety.

Another function of our minds is to assess whether something falls in the category of pleasure or pain. We're constantly monitoring events to make this simple, black-or-white evaluation. The general idea is to maximize our pleasure and to minimize our pain. And there's the rub. Our minds organize our experiences into what is good or bad for us. Our minds also use this same strategy to set up good/bad dichotomies for evaluating other people and their behavior. When we listen to that and follow what our mind is telling us, we end up going down the road to judgment and anger.

# HOW THE MIND MANUFACTURES ANGER

The prefrontal cortex—that part of our brain that uses language to evaluate experience—can literally manufacture anger by using the faculties of judgment, attribution, and assumed intent. Here's how these functions work to generate anger feelings and behavior.

## Judgment

Judgment is the natural spillover of the mind's tendency to categorize experience in black-or-white terms. With judgment, your mind is using the same strategies it has used to evaluate experiences as pleasurable or painful, safe or dangerous. Now, though, it's judging other people and their behavior as right or wrong. This is a critically important shift. With judgment, your mind is declaring something or someone to be absolutely and objectively good or bad. When the mind makes judgments, experience is no longer about subjective feelings of pleasure and pain; it is about the intrinsic moral worth of your experiences and the people around you. You compare them to a standard of what should be. And if they don't measure up to your standard, you may begin to get angry.

## Bill and Emma's Story

Bill and Emma are an example of how simple pleasure/pain evaluations can be transformed into good/bad judgments— and a pile of anger. Emma was working a lot of overtime on a research and development project at her laboratory. Bill missed her and felt lonely on the nights she worked late. It was a little painful rattling around the house by himself. Plus, Bill sensed that he and Emma weren't as close as they used to be; their relationship was starting to feel seriously disconnected.

At first, none of these evaluations made Bill angry. They sometimes made him feel sad, anxious, and fearful of losing her. But then he started turning them into good/bad judgments, thinking it was wrong of Emma to selfishly put her career above her relationship with him; that she shouldn't have agreed to all the overtime; that she was wrong to let their relationship "die on the vine." Bill's painful loneliness was transformed through judgment into moral outrage, faultfinding, and blame. Eventually Bill had it out with Emma for "destroying their lives," and threatened divorce.

Black-and-white judgments force you into the psychological straitjacket of a good/bad universe—the right way, the only way. You then can't see beyond it, because judgment masks your ability to connect with other dimensions of reality. The mask of judgment blocks your ability to recognize the complex needs, fears, and hopes that motivate other people—needs, fears, and hopes that are not very different from your own.

### Toxic Labeling

A second form of judgment is called toxic labeling. Here your mind transforms the very normal process of recognizing and labeling experience into a series of global judgments: people are stupid, incompetent, crazy, lazy, and so on. Toxic labels are, at the core, an indictment of worth used to legitimize anger and revenge. They are difficult to shake once applied.

## *George and Emilio's Story*

George and Emilio offer an example of how our minds will convert something that's merely painful into anger-cranking toxic labels. The two men repair underground phone lines, but Emilio has started complaining that George always seems to assign himself the easier jobs. So Emilio told George, "We got to be more fifty-fifty, man. You got to get down in the hole more, get a little dirty. I don't wanna be the only one in the hole, man."

George felt hurt, and a little ashamed. But his mind turned the pain into a judgment about another person. "Emilio's a controlling asshole. He's got a big mouth, always running it about something. Screw him." Once George turned Emilio into a big mouth, he could get angry and dismiss him.

## Attribution—The Blame Game

Our mind is structured to attribute underlying causes to events. We seek to discover the why of things. This drive is the basis of scientific thought and work. For example, Ben Franklin's desire to understand electricity led to his famous experiment with lightning, and eventually the entire power grid.

The natural tendency to make cause-and-effect connections can go sour when we have a painful experience (effect); our minds work to figure out why and then look for someone to blame (cause). Instead of thinking "Something's wrong, I'll find the source and fix it," we get trapped in the blame game. "Something's wrong (I'm in pain). I'll find who did this to me, then I'll attack them till *they* fix it."

Notice how blame keeps you helpless, because you're now depending on the other person to solve *your* problem. And you may use anger flowing from the blame game as a tool to coerce other people.

Blaming is a major source of human misery. It doesn't undo the past, nor does it fix the pain. What it does do is keep you stuck and alienated from the very people who could help you live a better life. So the problems—and your pain—continue. And your anger grows from episodic to chronic.

Escaping from the blame game requires that you take responsibility for yourself. When you're in pain, you need to be the agent of change. Looking around to see who's responsible won't help here. You and you alone are responsible for your experience. Blame keeps you from seeing this simple fact. It leaves you waiting to be helped, wanting, desperate to be rescued and vindicated. All of this fuels more blame, because the source of help and responsibility begins and ends with you.

## Assumed Intent—Becoming Mind Readers

Since we're wired to organize experience into cause and effect, we hate ambiguity. We are especially disturbed when other people do things we don't understand. Our minds try to solve these mysteries with something called "assumed intent."

Assumed intent is our effort to explain ambiguous behavior in others by trying to guess their intentions, feelings, and motives—essentially mind-reading. The trouble is we're often wrong. And since the intentions and motives we guess at are usually negative, we get angry for nothing.

## Lenny and Shirley's Story

Lenny and Shirley are an example of where mind reading can lead us. Lenny was spending more and more time in his study working on his computer. He said he was working on a project, but Shirley suspected he was playing Karmageddon or one of the other equally "stupid" games he has loaded on his hard drive. Three weeks into the "project," Shirley concluded that Lenny was deliberately withdrawing and punishing her because she bought a table he thought was too expensive. She eventually confronted Lenny, saying, "This is just a bullshit manipulation, just because you didn't get your way. Why don't you grow up?"

At that point, Lenny handed her a stack of prints. "I loaded them on Photoshop," he said. "Our trips for the last five years. I've been learning to crop and enhance the shots; now I'm arranging them in albums. It was going to be a surprise."

The assumption of intent can turn into a real nightmare when we get it wrong. And getting it wrong is exactly what we often do.

## How the Compulsion to Evaluate Affects Communication

Barriers to healthy communication are a direct outgrowth of the mind's tendencies to judge, blame, and assume intent—collectively, the compulsion to evaluate. These tendencies put up walls and turn people who are simply different from us, or who disagree with us, into adversaries. The mind wants to label them as wrong and/or bad. The mind tells you they are misguided, stupid, sinful. You may feel compelled to show them their errors. Whether the issue is sexual behavior or political convictions, or something as benign as washing the dishes, the outcome is the same: people who are different, who do things differently, or who disagree arouse anger and must be vanquished, beaten. In a right-versus-wrong universe, there is little room for much else, including the possibility that you (not they) may be mistaken or wrong. The angry mind is a closed mind that leaves little space for doubt, second thoughts, and other possibilities.

The compulsion to evaluate is the source of all defensiveness. Instead of exploring and seeking truth, your words are like soldiers trying to hold the perimeter. You fight off the assault of new ideas. You machine-gun the merest hint that you've got it wrong. Conversations are about winners and losers. Being right means being the winner, and so you use any kind of verbal pyrotechnics to avoid defeat. Losing in this system would mean you are mistaken, vulnerable, or worse—that at the very core you are bad.

There are two additional impacts that follow the compulsion to evaluate. The first outcome has to do with the fact that evaluation, by definition, involves wearing emotional blinders. These blinders leave you so consumed with defending your territory that you likely miss what's really going on. You don't see when others are hurt or needing validation or trying desperately to connect with you. You ignore vital information, including your own deeply felt pains and hurts, because it has nothing to do with winning.

Take Stewart, for example. He was so busy trying to convince Monica that her friend Tammy was "trailer trash," that he didn't hear this important communication: "At least Tammy likes me. She thinks I'm something. She thinks I'm cool." Oops! Stewart wasn't listening to Monica's need for validation. She dumped him three weeks later.

A second way evaluation hurts your relationships is that it keeps you from seeing life through another person's eyes. Your sense of perspective is greatly diminished or skewed. You're unable to connect with what other people know and understand, including what you may learn from them via their life experiences, pains, hurts, disappointments, joys, and perspective about the world. The blinders keep all of this from view. Why? Because the other person is different. So your mind simply makes him or her wrong. This ultimately hurts your ability to connect with people, learn from them, and be supported and nurtured.

## How the Compulsion to Evaluate Creates Resentment

Judging, blaming, and assuming are mental habits that are made worse by rumination. When you ruminate, you get stuck in cognitive loops, endlessly recycling the past through the same good/bad judgments, the same toxic labels. Over and over, you play tapes in your head of what someone did or said, blaming them for hurting you. The result is chronic resentment and a growing need for revenge. You feel righteous, strong. You imagine justice finally being done.

But what comes of this? Does the pain or hurt ever really get better? Is the relationship somehow healed? In reality, nothing changes. The rumination provides a moment of relief—an assertion of one's rightness, a shining fantasy of revenge. But the long-term emotional consequence is to feel hopeless and stuck. The resentment deepens; the pain just goes on and overflows into other areas of your life.

## How the Compulsion to Evaluate Triggers Destructive Behavior

The more we ruminate, and the more we believe and buy into our evaluative ruminations, the stronger the impulse gets to hurt others. In truth, evaluations are just mental constructs. They are no more real than Darth Vader; no truer than a fantasy of winning the lottery. Hitler's minister of propaganda, Joseph Goebbels, said if you tell a big enough lie often enough, people will believe it. Judgments and blame work the same way. If you keep ruminating, keep repeating the same thing to yourself, you can come to believe just about anything.

As you deepen your belief in a negative evaluation, when you really buy into it the judgment, it then takes on a life of its own. It starts to require action. Something must be said to set the offending person straight; something must be done to slap them awake so they'll finally see the error of their ways. A phenomenon psychologists call *emotional reasoning* starts to take control.

Emotional reasoning goes like this: "If I feel pain, someone must have done it to me. If someone did this to me, I have to hit them back so hard that they never hurt me again." This is schoolyard logic, the same kind of thinking that gets a lot of kids beat up. It's the same logic that motivates drive-by shootings and destroys friendships and marriages: "I'm hurt, you did it, you're bad, and I'll pay you back."

When the mind decides that others are bad and wrong, when the mind obsesses about revenge, there's often no end to it. You can end up with situations like the street fights in Beirut, the hatred and violence between Protestants and Catholics in Northern Ireland or between Hamas and Jews in the Middle East, and the war in Iraq. The will to inflict damage goes on and on, and it can quickly get out of control. Inflicting damage becomes all that matters, all that motivates. The costs are high and the suffering is huge.

## WHAT TO DO

Your mind evaluates and labels things to assign significance to events in your life. This is what minds do. It is a natural, normal process and often quite helpful. The trick is to take your mind less seriously, to watch it work without believing everything it says. This is easier said than done.

When your mind speaks with judgment, it speaks loudly. And when you try not to listen, it speaks even louder. It would be naive to assume that simply telling you to stop believing what your mind says would work to help you take your mind less seriously. You may have even tried this already.

One of the keys to becoming less ruled by what your mind tells you is to learn the skill of watching your mind. You can do it, but it takes time and practice. Your mind didn't start throwing evaluations at you overnight. It's been going on for a long lifetime. The skill of watching your mind will take practice and commitment, but it's a powerful tool for changing your experience of anger.

To get you started, we recommend that you go through the four exercises described below: mind watching, separating thoughts from anger feelings, riding the wave of anger, and compassion in the dark. Each exercise will help you detach from the compulsion to evaluate and believe those evaluations. We suggest you do them one at a time to see which ones work best for you.

It's important to give yourself enough time with each exercise. These exercises are not magic bullets. They require practice. A good starting point is to set aside at least ten to fifteen minutes each day to practice an exercise. Give each of them a few days of practice before moving on to the next. A bit later on we'll talk about applying some of the skills learned from these exercises in your daily life.

## MIND WATCHING

Mind watching requires you to be a true observer of your consciousness. Here's how you do it.

Start by taking a series of slow, deep breaths. Keep this up through the entire exercise. Imagine that your mind is a medium-sized white room with two doors. Thoughts come in through the front door and leave out the back door. Pay close attention to each thought as it enters. Now label the thought as either judging or nonjudging.

Watch the thought until it leaves. Don't try to analyze or hold onto it. Don't believe or disbelieve it. Just acknowledge having the thought. It's just a moment in your mind, a brief visitor to the white room. If you find yourself judging yourself for having the thought, notice *that*. Do not argue with your mind's judgment. Just notice it for what it is and label it "judging—there is judging." The key to this exercise is to notice the judgmental thoughts rather than getting caught up in them. You'll know if you're getting caught up in them by your emotional reactions and by how long you keep the thoughts in the room.

Keep breathing; keep watching; keep labeling. A thought is just a thought. And you are much more than that thought. Each thought doesn't require you to react; it doesn't make you do anything; it doesn't mean you are less of a person. As an observer of your thoughts as they pass in and out of the white room, let them have their brief life. They are fine the way they are, including the judging thoughts. The important thing is to let them leave when they are ready to go and then greet and label the next thought—and the next.

Continue this exercise until you feel a real emotional distance from your thoughts. Wait until even the judgments are just a moment in the room—no longer important, no longer requiring action.

## SEPARATING THOUGHTS FROM ANGER FEELINGS

This exercise will help you learn to detach your thoughts from angry feelings.

Start by recalling a recent situation where you felt angry. Try to visualize what happened, what was said. Take some time to carefully build a picture of the event. Now remember some of the thoughts you had during the episode. As you recall what you were thinking, notice if the actual feeling of anger is starting to return. If it is, that's good. Let it happen.

Keep focusing on the judgmental or blaming thoughts connected to the incident. Really get into them. And if your anger feels a little sharper, a little stronger, that's fine, too.

Now go back to the white room. Imagine that your anger is hurling those judgmental and blaming thoughts through the front door. Take a deep breath. Inhale slowly, then let your whole body relax as you release the breath. Keep this up while you start watching your mind. Observe and label the thoughts. Watch each thought from a distance—without believing or getting entangled in it. Don't make the thought bigger or smaller, don't agree or disagree. Just watch and breathe, noticing that the thought eventually leaves and a new one takes its place. Keep this up until you feel a growing distance from the thoughts—and perhaps from the anger itself.

Your anger and judgmental thoughts each tend to trigger the other, escalating in a rising spiral. But you can interrupt that process by simply observing and labeling your thoughts. They will, after a while, feel very separate from the anger, detached. And they will lose the power to make rage burn hotter. What you can learn by practicing this exercise is that you can become an observer of your thoughts. This will help you see just how automatically your mind reacts to all that you experience. It might also help you not get tangled up so much in your thoughts.

## Emotions Are Like Waves

Imagine for a moment an ocean wave as it approaches shore. It's steep and tall, but hasn't yet crested into a breaker. Now imagine the wave nearing a little group of gulls floating on the water. The birds don't fly away. They simply ride up the facing slope, round the top, and drift down the long back of the wave.

That's what you can learn to do with anger. All emotions are wavelike and time limited. They ebb and flow. They slowly build up, and get bigger and more powerful. Eventually, the wave will reach its peak and dissipate. Anger comes and goes in a similar way. It doesn't last forever, even if it feels like it will.

We encourage you to ride the wave of your anger. You must initially face the steep leading edge. At this point, the wave is tall and scary. You may feel that it will go on forever, that you may somehow drown. Finally the emotion reaches its zenith; instead of getting stronger it starts to recede. You may feel yourself slipping down the back of the wave, the anger quieting.

That's how emotions work if you don't try to control or block them, if you let the wave run its course. But if you try to fight the wave, if you refuse to ride it out, something very different happens. You'll never get over the top. You stay stuck on the wave's leading edge, and it keeps pushing you. Eventually—sometimes after hours or days—the emotional wave crests and crashes. Then you're caught churning helplessly beneath the surface of the water, at the mercy of the full force of the crush and undertow.

## RIDING THE WAVE OF ANGER

Right now you have a chance to learn to ride the wave of your anger rather than be tumbled about by it. Think of a recent situation where you felt mistreated and upset. Visualize the scene; try to recall any irritating things that were done or said. Notice your judging or blaming thoughts. Keep focusing on the upsetting scene, as well as on the judgments you made about it. Let your anger rise till it's a four or five on a scale of one to ten.

Good. Now go back to the white room. Observe your thoughts. Label the judgments. The thoughts aren't right or wrong, true or false. Acknowledge their presence without trying to control or change them, without trying to push them away. Breathe deeply; keep watching your mind.

At the same time, notice the emotional wave in the room with you. Be aware of the point where your anger stops climbing. Feel it leveling off and starting to diminish. Experience the slow ride down the back of the wave. Accept wherever you are on the wave. Don't hasten to get past it. It moves at its own speed—all you can do is let go and let it carry you.

Just watch your thoughts entering and leaving the white room, and notice the progress of the wave, nothing more. Keep watching until the anger has completely passed.

## FINDING COMPASSION IN THE DARK

Imagine that it's night. You are in a field with hundreds of unseen people. On one edge of the field is a cliff—it would be an extraordinary and terrifying fall. The cliff is really everyone's worst fear—death, shame, failure, aloneness, loss, helplessness. No one can see it. No one knows where it is.

Now imagine that you and all the other people in the field will live your lives there. You must find food, love, and companionship in the darkness. You must keep moving yet somehow avoid the cliff. You're always a little afraid, always uncertain, because the darkness never lifts. And you must find all that you need to live without falling into the abyss.

This is our human condition. People cope in different ways. Some race headlong; some hesitate to make the smallest step. Some cling; some push others away for fear of being dragged past the edge. Some give up; some seek to understand, forever trying to pierce the darkness. Some demand help; some comfort themselves by trying to help others.

Close your eyes and be in the field. Feel how we all struggle there. Feel how we try to move, to take care of ourselves, while always sensing the presence of the cliff. Everyone walks that dark field; everyone is scared; everyone is doing the best they can.

Now think of someone you care for (such as your partner, your child, or your best friend). Keep observing your thoughts and feelings while imagining that person walking around in the dark field. They are hoping not to fall, just like you. Be aware of their fear and struggle. As you do so, the wish may arise in you to help them, to be by their side, and perhaps to comfort them. That is all fine. Keep holding the image while watching each thought and feeling come and go.

Now think of someone who makes you angry; watch the judgmental thoughts that start to form. Keep observing your thoughts and feelings while imagining that person navigating the dark field. They are hoping not to fall, just like you and the person you care for. Be aware of their fear and struggle. Is it different from yours? Keep holding the image of their fear and struggle while watching each arriving thought and feeling. This may be more difficult to do, because you don't like that person very much and you may keep getting caught up in judgmental thoughts. Still, keep holding the image of their fear and struggle while watching each arriving thought and feeling.

Notice that your task in this exercise is not to stop your anger or your judgmental thoughts. There's no reason to change what you experience. Your experience is what it is, and it does not harm you. But what you are doing here is something extraordinary that you may have never done before: you are adding compassionate awareness to your experience, so that your anger is balanced with full appreciation of the challenge of being human.

## THE TAKE-HOME MESSAGE

The most important thing we hope you take from this chapter is that your mind—those good/bad judgments and toxic labels—has a powerful impact on your emotions. But if you observe instead of trying to control your mind, if you watch instead of trying to control your feelings, your anger will paradoxically stop controlling you. Judgments are a necessary and inescapable part of living. They'll always be there. But you no longer have to be attached to them or believe them. They're ultimately just thoughts to notice and let go.

# WEEK 5
## Learning about how my mind creates anger

**Points to ponder:** Minds will always do what minds do. I can bring compassion to what my evaluative mind comes up with and learn to ride the wave of anger.

**Questions to consider:** Do I really have to believe all the judgments that my mind dishes up for me all the time? Am I willing to learn to see judgments as thoughts and not act on what they say?

# Chapter 6

# Getting Out of the Anger Trap with Acceptance

*Acceptance simply means willingness to see things as they are, deeply, truthfully, and completely. This attitude sets the stage for acting in the most potent and healthy way in your life, no matter what is happening.*

—Jeffrey Brantley

Many people feel trapped by their anger, unable to retreat or withdraw once their anger feelings are triggered. It's like being launched on auto-pilot into a tight space where there doesn't seem to be any room for other choices or other ways of responding.

This chapter is about making room for other choices. The first step to that end is for you to recognize the feelings and fears that underlie your anger.

# ACCEPTANCE AS AN ALTERNATIVE

Although recognition is an important start, it will not suffice to get you out of the anger trap. You will also need to learn a new way of responding to your anger: approaching it—and the feelings underlying it—with acceptance and compassion. Taking the path of acceptance goes against the grain; it's counterintuitive when you're feeling angry. But it can liberate you from remaining stuck in the anger trap with all your old behavior patterns that don't work. Meeting your pain with compassion cuts off anger at the root, leaving it unable to grow and spread. Practicing acceptance is an act of kindness toward yourself that allows you to heal and move on with your life.

## Passive Acceptance Is Resignation

There are two kinds of acceptance: passive and active. One is about giving up and losing, and the other is about action and doing. Many people associate acceptance with giving up, giving in, and losing out. This type of passive acceptance, or resignation, is not what we want you to do, because it keeps you stuck. Resignation is when you let anger (a feeling you cannot control) guide your actions (which you can control). Instead, we want you to muster the courage to act and change.

## Active Acceptance Is Compassion

Active acceptance is quite different. We think of active acceptance as compassion in action. It involves softening your mind and heart to the anger and hostility in you and connecting with them in the present moment. You do this by letting go of the struggle with your inner experience of anger, hostility, and hurt. You let go by bringing kindness and gentle attention to unwanted anger-related thoughts and feelings, by simply allowing them to be there without suppressing, changing, or acting on them. Our colleague Jeffrey Brantley (2003) describes this process as becoming a friend to yourself and to your anger.

Doing so is challenging and will take a commitment on your part. There is no quick way to get there, no magic acceptance pill. But you can learn compassion in action gradually, over time, by practicing the exercises in this book and staying committed to learning this useful skill, even when you experience the inevitable setbacks in your progress.

## Acceptance Makes Room for Choices

We focus on acceptance for practical reasons: struggling with anger doesn't work, and acceptance creates space for new beginnings, new ways of responding. When you stop wasting time and energy trying to change anger-related thoughts and feelings, you're free to take control of what you *can* control—what you do with your hands, feet, and mouth in response to what you experience.

## CHINESE FINGER TRAPS

To get a sense of what we mean by creating space, imagine playing with one of those Chinese finger traps that you may have played with as a child. A finger trap is a tube of woven straw about five inches long and half an inch wide. Perhaps you can find one in a novelty store and do the exercise for real. If not, just imagine doing it.

During this exercise, you pick up the finger trap and slide one index finger into each end of the tube. After you fully insert your fingers, try to pull them out. You'll notice that the tube catches and tightens. You experience some discomfort as the tube squeezes your fingers and reduces circulation. You may feel a little confused, because pulling out of the tube seems the most obvious, natural way to respond. Yet it doesn't work. The harder you try to pull yourself out of the trap, the more stuck you are. That is exactly how the anger trap that we've been talking about throughout this book works. Trying to reduce anger feelings by responding with anger behavior constrains your life and limits your space for making choices.

As with the finger trap, our instinctive solutions to anger feelings (for example, lashing out at people who hurt us) often turn out to be no solutions at all. In fact, these so-called solutions create even bigger problems. Pulling away from anger may seem like a natural and logical way to free yourself from the anger trap. But your experience with anger tells you that this struggle has only brought you more discomfort and life problems.

The good news is that there is an alternative that does work and is supported by our research (Eifert and Heffner 2003). To get there, you have to do something that goes against your instincts. Instead of pulling out, you have to push your fingers *in*. This move will definitely give you more space to move around—more wiggle room.

In the context of anger, acceptance is doing something seemingly counterintuitive to get yourself unstuck from where you are with your life right now. It is leaning *into* your pain and anger rather than pulling away from them. You do this by acknowledging your discomfort and anger feelings and making room for that discomfort, allowing it to be, without doing anything about it or getting involved with it, and without trying to make it go away. If you do this, you'll suddenly find that you have more room to move around and live your life.

## THE FOUR STEPS OF ACCEPTANCE

Using acceptance, you're going to meet the fire that fuels anger with active compassion and kindness. To get there involves a commitment to learning four interrelated steps: acknowledging your anger; accepting the situation as it is; identifying the hurt, fear, and judgment; and responding with forgiveness and compassion.

### Step 1: Acknowledge Your Anger

First you need to learn to acknowledge that you are angry when you're feeling angry. If you don't recognize or acknowledge anger, you'll never find out what is fueling it. And, if you don't know what is fueling your anger, you will have no way to learn new ways of relating to the source of anger within you. So, you need to start here.

The next time you sense anger coming—when you feel the emo-tions surging and the evaluative mind in high gear—just acknowl-edge, "There it is. There is anger. I'm angry and I need to take care of it." Taking care of your anger feeling does not mean acting on it. We'll show you exactly how you can attend to it in step 4. At this point, it's only important to acknowledge that you are indeed angry—and that you stay with that feeling. Don't try to pull away from it or make it go away.

## Step 2: Accept the Situation as It Is

Learn to acknowledge that the situation is what it is. Your mind may not accept the reality of whatever is happening; it may tell you that things shouldn't be the way they are. If you keep insisting "But things should be different" or "But people should treat me with more respect," you'll get stuck waiting for someone else to fix the problem. You need to accept the situation *as is* and take full responsibility to make any changes you can.

To do so, you'll have to recognize your mind machine at work. You can recognize it more easily if you label what it's doing: "There is my mind, judging," "There is my mind, blaming," "There is my mind, scheming to get even." Remember, your mind is good at creating anger. It's important for you to learn not to believe or do what your mind is telling you, or what your body appears to be telling you when you feel like you're about to explode.

You can learn to not to buy into your mind machine by recogniz-ing and acknowledging your thoughts and feelings for what they are. For instance, when such thoughts pop up as "This jerk could have paid more attention" or "She really shouldn't have done that," you can say to yourself, "I'm having the thought that this jerk could have paid more attention," and "I'm having the thought that she really shouldn't have done that." In regard to feelings you can say, "I'm having the feeling that I'm about to explode" or "I'm having the feeling that [insert whatever you typically feel]."

These admittedly awkward and cumbersome labeling and lan-guage habits will help you recognize thoughts as thoughts and feelings as feelings. We will also use them in several later exercises. They help you create some space between yourself and your anger thoughts and feelings so you can start becoming response-able and changing what you can change.

## Step 3: Identify the Hurt, Fear, and Judgment

This step is about identifying what is fueling the flames of anger—the hurt and judgment that underlie it—so that you can start the process of letting go of them. It's about discovering which of your buttons has been pushed, what hurts you, or what's scaring you. It's particularly important to notice what evaluative statements your mind machine is coming up with about you, the people in your life, and the current situation.

Let's look at the experience of David, a thirty-three-year-old engineer working for a construction company. David made several important discoveries about his struggle with anger.

## David's Story

I've always had anger, but lately I've come to see it as a problem. I get angry about everything, and I fixate on whatever got me angry. I'm fuming mad! It's the little things that tick me off. It seems like not one day can go by without me being angry at something. I feel like I really hurt the people around me with my blowups. And doing that makes me feel bad about myself. I've always disliked angry people, and it seems like everything I don't like, I am. I don't want people to avoid me or think of me as being mean because I can't control my anger. I've put so much effort into dealing with my doubts and insecurities about myself. For the last six years, life has felt like a chore. I can't get through a day without feeling sick or scared. My life feels like a job because I'm always working so hard at it. But I'm still alone and get paid only in Pepto-Bismol. I'm angry because I don't know where all these bad feelings come from. I'm angry because I don't know how to fix them. I'm also mad because I thought they would be gone by now, given how much I've worked on them. Now I'm scared that I'll always have these feelings about myself. When will I be free?

This sad story may resonate with the experiences of many people who struggle with problem anger. Yet David is ahead of the game in one important respect: he discovered that being angry is very much about him rather than other people. Being angry has to do with his negative feelings about himself (for example, doubts about his abilities) and his tendency to beat himself up for having those feelings and not being able to resolve his anger.

The following exercise is about helping you recognize what fuels your anger so you can learn to accept the sources of your anger and start taking better care of them. Be mindful that the quality of pain and hurt can change from anger episode to anger episode, from situation to situation, and from person to person.

This exercise will take a bit longer than the previous ones. Since you can't read and close your eyes at the same time, we recommend that you read through the following script a few times first. Then close your eyes and follow the instructions. You can also record the script on an audio cassette and play it back to yourself while you practice.

## THE ANGER ARMOR

Go ahead and get in a comfortable position in your chair. Sit upright with your feet flat on the floor, your arms and legs uncrossed, and your hands resting in your lap (palms up or down, whichever is more comfortable). Close your eyes and take a few deep breaths. Relax. Allow your body to rest without drifting off to sleep.

To get started, we would like you to re-create a real image of yourself being angry. Think of a recent example when someone pushed your buttons and you got angry—perhaps you can refer back to the anger map exercise in chapter 3. Think of the moment. Notice the anger coming and all the surging bodily changes. Notice the trigger thoughts your evaluative mind comes up with. Enter into the whole image as best as you can. Watch as the feeling grows and notice how quickly it is there in full force. Also notice how quickly you want to do something about the anger feeling, and what it makes you want to do. For instance, do you have any impulses to speak out or act on your anger? Be aware of the evaluative thoughts you're having about the event or yourself. Hold those thoughts clearly in your mind, put them into sentences, and watch them as if you were watching them in a mirror. Keep focusing on what you're feeling. Notice how your body and mind harden, consumed by anger. It's everywhere.

Now imagine for a moment that all these harsh, judgmental thoughts, intense anger feelings, and strong impulses are connected. They form one big piece of armor—the kind of heavy armor that knights used to wear to protect their whole body. You're in it. Feel how heavy it is and how hard it is for you to move.

Anger is like wearing heavy armor. The armor masks the pain and vulnerability we all have by simple virtue of being human. Behind the pain, there may be something you're attached to, something you're holding on to. What is it in your case? See whether you can identify what you're trying to protect or defend with your anger armor. There might be feelings of guilt . . . shame . . . hurt . . . fear . . . loss . . . helplessness . . . rejection . . . inadequacy . . . unworthiness. Or perhaps it's your reputation, image, the approval of others, rules, beliefs, past mistakes, missed opportunities, or decisions that did not go right. It could also be that you fear losing a person, or a possession, or place, or money. See if you can identify what exactly fuels your anger.

Every time the pain and hurt touch the inside of the armor, they corrode it. Your armor begins to weaken, pit, and rust from the inside. And as it rusts, you begin to feel vulnerable. To keep yourself protected and safe, you've been fixing the rusty parts and holes that start to show through by welding new patches of metal onto the old ones, so the armor gets heavier and heavier. It weighs on you, dragging you down physically, emotionally, psychologically, and spiritually. You don't seem to be able to do much except clank around in your armor. The burden is tremendous. Movement is difficult.

Next, imagine yourself stepping out of the armor and putting it right next to you. Imagine yourself standing there just looking at your anger armor. If it helps, try to visualize looking at yourself and the armor in a mirror. You and anyone around you can finally see who you are. You're standing there with your naked emotions and imperfections for everyone to see. You're exposed and vulnerable. See whether you can stay with this feeling.

Notice how much lighter you feel now. Without the armor, you're no longer tied down by all that weight. You can move more easily and more quickly than before. Your hands, arms, and feet are free. By stepping out of the armor and just observing it, you have gained flexibility and freedom of movement.

The lightness that comes from acceptance won't develop overnight. It's like learning to ride a bike—sometimes you will fall. You will occasionally reach again for the armor and spend your time patching and repairing it, because it makes you feel safe when hurts show up. As you learn acceptance, your need to hide from pain and hurt inside the anger armor will gradually decrease. Accepting yourself and being patient with all your flaws, weaknesses, strengths, and talents—the whole package—involves taking many small steps in that general direction. You're on the right track as long as you keep practicing and stay committed to that path.

## Step 4: Respond with Forgiveness and Compassion

Acceptance is about opening up to the pain inside you with kindness, love, patience, and compassion. For this reason, we need to address the pains and hurts—what anger is helping you protect. We're not going after your pain with cheap fixes or more patches. Instead, we're going to expose it for what it is and meet it with acceptance, compassion, and patience.

### Accept and Forgive Yourself First

Accepting yourself is the most important and often the most difficult first step. It pulls the rug out from underneath your anger and helps you focus your energy on what is important to you and what you can do and change. The prize here is a life—your life!

It's useful to acknowledge having feelings of anger, worthlessness, and failure, but putting yourself down for them only leads to more resentment and self-hatred. That is never helpful.

Take the case of Jillian, a thirty-seven-year-old mother of two daughters (seven and ten years old). Her father sexually and physically abused her until her parents separated when she was twelve. She went to college, majored in English, and started to work for a regional newspaper where she met her husband. They divorced two years ago. Jillian came into therapy after a social worker suggested she seek help with her anger problem if she didn't want to lose custody of her kids:

## Jillian's Story

I don't understand why I get so mad at my two daughters. I love them and I don't want to hurt them. I know what it's like to be beaten by a parent, but I've hit my kids on several occasions anyway. And now I might lose them. So here I am getting mad at my daughters when I am the one who's to blame. I'm the one who should be beaten up. I couldn't give my husband what he was looking for, and so he left me. And to this day, I'm wondering if I did something to make my dad do what he did, because he never abused my younger sister. Deep down, I have this fear that I am just no good; no good as a daughter, wife, or mother.

You read what happened to David when he continued to buy into his evaluative mind. Now the same thing is playing out with Jillian. The story has changed, but the problem is the same. Jillian has come to believe the harsh judgments of her mind. Both David and Jillian continue to struggle with what happened in their past. And they struggle with their present thoughts and feelings. It's like an emotional double whammy: First they struggle with their fears and doubts about themselves. Then they get angry at themselves and beat themselves up over the mere fact of having all those unwanted feelings, along with their perceived failure to control them.

Jeffrey Brantley (2003) wrote that we often don't recognize what our mind machines do to us. Our evaluative minds provide us a constant supply of judgments and self-critical statements. It may seem that you've always had these thoughts. Most of the time you may not even notice them, at least not until the feelings or the comments become uncomfortably harsh. Until you pay attention to them, you may not know where they come from. But when you start believing those comments and acting on them, you become your own worst stressor.

If you want to break the vicious cycle of anger and aggression, you must recognize that your mind machine is at work here (just like in step 2). When you catch and observe the mind doing its judging, you've taken the first step toward being kinder to yourself and others. Recognizing judgments for what they are—thoughts and nothing but thoughts—will help you let go of judging and blaming yourself and others. This is also the moment when you start accepting yourself as you are, with your flaws and all that has happened to you. Remember, you cannot stop your mind dishing up evaluative statements. What you can learn is to see them for what they are and relate to them in a different way.

### How to Take Care of Your Anger Baby

You probably have some old wounds—from losses, unfair treat-ment by others, perhaps even real abuse. The hurt may be old and the wound may have a scab on it. When someone hurts you and pushes your buttons, they're ripping that scab right off to expose the open wound. It doesn't matter whether your mind says this was intentional or not. The wound was there anyway. You are in touch with an aspect of yourself that you may prefer not to know. This is a golden opportu-nity to embrace it with compassion and acceptance.

Jillian, in the story above, was frustrated over the fact that she was treating her children the same way she was treated by her father. People who have been hurt themselves often continue to inflict pain on others because they have not taken care of their wounds. They have not allowed their wounds to heal. If you don't take care of your wounds, you may pass them on to your children, spouse, friends, colleagues at work, and other people in your life. Hurt and anger can be recycled many times.

Take a moment to think about what you do when something is physically wrong with you—like a scraped knee, or a problem with your stomach, your back, or your teeth. We suspect that you stop whatever you're doing and attend to your injury or illness. And that is the right thing to do.

We suggest you do the same with your open anger wound, and attend to all those feelings of shame, fear, and guilt, all that blaming of yourself and others. Further beating is not a good way to treat an open wound and help it heal. You'd never treat a bleeding knee in such a harsh way. So if you want to break the cycle of anger, you have to start by taking better care of your anger—by being kind to yourself. You can do this by no longer buying into all the judging and blaming your mind machine comes up with. Anger is not the enemy. Other people are not the enemy. Just like your physical body, your anger and emotional pain are part of you. When you're angry, you can turn your attention back to yourself and take good care of your anger. That is what we mean by embracing anger with compassion.

You can learn to take care of yourself, your anger, and your wounds. You don't need to rely on other people to change first. Thich Nhat Hanh (2001) developed a powerful and yet simple exercise to help you practice compassion with yourself. It shows you how to take care of your anger as if it were your sick baby in need of your love and attention.

## GIVING YOURSELF LOVING KINDNESS

Remember when you were a little child and you had a fever? You felt bad. So a parent or caregiver came and gave you aspirin or other medicine. This may have helped, but it was nothing like having your mom there. You didn't feel better until your mother came and put her hand on your burning forehead. That felt so good! To you, her hand was like the hand of a goddess. When she touched you with her hand, a lot of freshness, love and compassion penetrated into your body. The hand of your mother is your own hand. Her hand is still alive in yours, if you know how to breathe in and out, to be mindful. Then, touching your forehead with your very own hand, you will see that your mother's hand is still there, touching your forehead. You will have the same energy of love and tenderness for yourself. (Hanh 2001, p. 33)

Like in the finger trap exercise, this is the time to take an unusual step and be open to what may happen. Here is what you can do: Close your eyes, touch your forehead, and think of your mother's hands touching you when you were young and sick. The kindness of her hand is alive in yours. And you can give that kindness to yourself right now.

If you didn't have a mother who was kind to you in this way, imagine another person who was kind to you as a child. Imagine how his or her hand felt.

## ACCEPTANCE AND PATIENCE

Acceptance and patience are very much related because both are about allowing what is to be there without judging or responding to it.

If you experience anger and you accept it, you are patient with it. Patience is the most effective antidote to anger. You can look at it this way: If anger is like poison from a venomous snake, patience is the antivenom that can heal you and keep you alive.

Let's say that someone pushed your buttons and criticized you. You feel the anger rising; your mind and body are quickly getting ready to defend, justify, blame, attack. What would being patient look like in this situation? Pema Chödrön captures it well:

> Patience has a quality of enormous honesty in it, but it also has a quality of not escalating things, allowing a lot of space for the other person to say what they want to say while you listen. You don't react to what you're feeling, even though inside you are reacting. You let the words go and just be there. When you practice patience, you're not repressing anger, you're just sitting there with it—going cold turkey with the aggression. You will really get to know anger and how it breeds violent words and actions. You will see the whole thing without acting it out . . . and you will be cultivating enormous courage. (2005 p. 34)

You can see that being patient has nothing to do with suppression. Far from it. Patience means that you are honest about the fact that you are angry. At the same time, you're doing nothing to feed your anger feelings and thoughts. You don't get involved with them or react to them. You don't argue with them. You also don't blame or criticize yourself for having them. You just let go of that whole internal dialogue. Acceptance paired with patience forms an entryway into a place where you can think about and react to your anger and other unwanted experiences in entirely new ways.

## Acceptance Is a Difficult and Valuable Choice

Acceptance and patience do not come easy or naturally for most of us. As we mentioned in chapter 5, your mind, with its evaluative language, tends to color your world with ideas of what is right or wrong. This is especially true when you're prone to anger and tangled up in a web of self-doubt, what-ifs, shoulds, and patterns of behavior designed to get you away from experiencing any of them.

You can, however, learn to be open to what is without con-
taminating the experience with your evaluations, justifications, and
reasons for what ought to be. This will take time and practice, but it
will eventually move you in a new, positive direction. So be patient
with yourself while you're learning about patience!

Acceptance and patience are ultimately about choices you make
every day. We can guarantee that an acceptance posture on one day
will not carry over to the next day. It's a choice you need to make
again and again. After a while it may seem like almost every moment
of your life you're making a choice: to open or close, to harden or
soften, to hold on or let go (Chödrön 2005). If the old pattern of
closing, hardening, and holding on to resentment has not worked for
you, it's time to open up, soften, and let go. There are exercises in
chapter 7 that will help you achieve this.

# DEBUNKING SOME MYTHS ABOUT ACCEPTANCE

Many people at first misunderstand what we mean by acceptance in
the context of anger. Before moving on to more acceptance exercises
in the next chapter, we want to take a few moments to debunk some of
the most common myths about acceptance.

## Myth 1: Acceptance Means Condoning Wrongdoing

This is probably the leading misconception about acceptance.
People fear that when they accept, they give approval to what is happening or has happened to them. Acceptance is not about approving,
liking, or condoning what is happening to you now or has happened to
you in the past. Acceptance is a matter of acknowledging and experiencing what happened in the past and what is happening in the
present moment without judging or getting all tangled up in that
experience.

Acceptance does not mean you sit still when someone harms you.
If anyone harms you now, you have every right to protect yourself from
further harm and do what it takes to be safe. Yet, holding on to old
hurts about past situations will never resolve those situations. They are

in the past, and you are in the present. You cannot change the past. You can only change how you respond to the past in the present.

You may ask, "Why should I let go of my anger and forgive those who harmed me?" The answer is simple and practical: Forgiving yourself and others is the only path to healing. If you don't let go and forgive others for the harm they did, they and their deeds will continue to haunt you, harm you, and have a hold on you. Every day you hang on to your resentment, you harm yourself one more time. So by not forgiving, you hurt no other person more than yourself. It's a form of self-torture; it continues to make the armor around you thicker, heavier, and more constraining. This is why we focus on forgiveness here and later on, in chapter 9. Acceptance means acknowledging what happened and letting go of blame and resentment. This is the way to reclaim your life where you live it—right here and now.

## Myth 2: Acceptance Is Weakness

Acceptance takes courage and strength. It is the harder path when compared with the tendency to give in or blow up. Noticing anger and the full strength of the emotion without acting it out is like riding a tiger. You may notice your mind criticizing and blaming both others and yourself. You may also notice feeling guilty about blaming when you "should" be accepting. It can be agonizing, because you feel bad about being so angry at the same time that you really are angry, and you can't drop it (Chödrön 2005).

Sitting with this energy and edginess without trying to suppress it or make it go away is the opposite of weakness. Staying with the anger and pain without acting on it or because of it is one of the most difficult things you will ever do. This decision is courageous, honest, open, compassionate, and empowering because it is liberating. When we ask clients who have made this choice to describe how acceptance feels to them, they often say things like "A burden has been lifted" or "I feel free and ready to move on."

## Myth 3: Acceptance Means Liking My Experience

It feels uncomfortable to experience anger, fear, insecurity, and hurt. In fact, it is really unpleasant. Acceptance is not about liking those feelings. It is a matter of no longer fighting with your experience or denying its reality. It just means seeing it for what it is rather than struggling against it. Again, it's like dropping the rope in a tug-of-war: Once you're no longer fighting the anger team, you free up energy—as well as your hands and feet—to create the life you want to live.

## Myth 4: Acceptance Is a Feeling

When you accept your experience, you respond differently to it. This is not just a feeling—it's a stance that will completely change your point of view. It's stepping back from your experience to develop a new way of relating with it that's guided by the kindness you have tucked away inside of you.

For instance, when you practice mindfulness exercises, you observe your anger and other feelings without judging, suppressing, or getting rid of them. It's like looking at your experiences as if they were playing out in a movie. You're not the movie. You are the observer of what is happening in the movie. Such skillful observation of life in the present moment, without judgment and with compassion, is an active response—just not in the way we usually think of being active (as in the running, fighting, struggling, and so forth that we described in chapter 4). Acceptance is a new posture toward your experiences—all of them—where you allow them to simply be as they are.

## Myth 5: Acceptance Means
## Diminished Responsibility

Acceptance is the highest form of response-ability you can take. By acknowledging and allowing your unwanted thoughts and emotions to be there rather than letting them dictate what you do, you actually increase your response-ability—your ability to take charge of your life!

## Myth 6: Acceptance Is a Clever Way
## to Manage Discomfort

Acceptance cannot prevent the pain of losing a loved one or getting hurt by another person. Feeling this type of pain is normal. No human being can escape such pain. It happens to all of us and is simply a function of living.

However, acceptance can prevent pain from turning into suffering. Pain turns into suffering when you don't accept the pain and hurt, when you don't acknowledge your pain, or when you struggle to get rid of it by lashing out at someone. Just as in the finger trap exercise, the discomfort increases the more you try to pull away from it.

It is this unnecessary suffering that mindful acceptance seeks to end. By practicing mindfulness exercises, you can gradually teach yourself to be less reactive to your evaluative mind and stay with emotional pain, rather than running away or trying to fix it. When the pain of anger shows up and you allow it in without struggle or reaction, you are free to act in ways that matter to you. The goal is to develop a place of calm above the storm, to promote health and vitality, and to foster caring kindness toward yourself first and then extend that to others.

## THE TAKE-HOME MESSAGE

By approaching anger thoughts and feelings with compassionate acceptance, you deprive your anger of the fuel it needs to burn. This will ultimately lower and cool the flames of anger. The prize for being more accepting, compassionate, and patient is that you become more flexible. You will be on anger autopilot less often. Acceptance increases your response-ability. It adds options to your life that are different from the same old programming you have grown accustomed to. It changes you by allowing you to be who you are *as you are* and by making you aware that you have control over what you do. Whether pain and hurt come or not is outside your control. How you respond to pain and hurt is one domain where you have choice. By staying with, and being patient with, your anger and hurt when they come, rather than running away from or attempting to fix them, you become free to focus on the life you want to live.

# WEEK 6
### Learning about acceptance

**Points to ponder:** Acceptance is a vital and courageous activity. Patience paired with acceptance can lead me to a new place.

**Questions to consider:** Am I willing to accept myself with all my flaws, weakness, and vulnerabilities? Am I willing to forgive others and myself so that I can move on and reclaim my life?

# Chapter 7

# Practicing Mindful Acceptance

*On all the tragic scene they stare. . . . Their eyes mid many*
*wrinkles, their eyes, their ancient, glittering eyes, are gay.*

—William Butler Yeats

In Yeats's great poem "Lapis Lazuli," three men on a high mountain
watch all the pain and loss and violent conflict in the world. They
observe it and feel it. Yet in the face of all this struggle, they see the
good. They know the gorgeous paradox of beauty and pain, loss and
love, reaching and failing.

This is mindful acceptance: watching the struggle without judging
it, feeling the pain without drowning in it, honoring the hurt without
becoming it. Mindful acceptance is not a feeling or an attitude. It

doesn't come from crystals, or insight, or some emotional apotheosis. Mindful acceptance is a skill—something that takes work to learn.

The skill of mindfulness, like anything else you get good at, is built on practice. It starts with easy steps and develops to include the most difficult situations in your life. Mindful acceptance is best practiced at home as you begin, in a comfortable, safe environment. As you get skilled at it, you can gradually expand to include more stressful, emotion-triggering situations, including those that involve anger.

The practice of mindful acceptance has three purposes. First, you learn to anchor yourself in the present moment, instead of in the hurts and violations of the past. As long as you live in the here and now, there is very little to be angry about. Second, mindful acceptance helps you let go of old control and avoidance strategies that only serve to make your anger worse. Third, the discipline of acceptance creates the psychological room to choose healthier responses to provocation. Instead of the automatic rage or blowup, you gain the flexibility to look for a response that doesn't damage your life and relationships.

# YOU ARE NOT YOUR ANGER

It is important to understand that you are not your anger. Anger is something you experience periodically. It explodes into your awareness and, after a while, it recedes. You are not the anger. You—the person who experiences and observes your life—are separate from your feelings of anger. Like every other thought or emotion, your anger struts for its moment on the stage, then slips into the wings. The only permanent, immutable thing is you—the audience, the watcher of your life.

We encourage you not to take your anger so seriously. It's just a moment in time, a wave on the sea of existence. You don't have to fight it—and you don't have to join it, either. Your task, the work of mindful acceptance, is to disentangle yourself from your anger, not to become your anger. Just let the wave of angry feeling come and go. Watch it from the safety of the shore—your strong, enduring self.

Here's another way to look at it: All your feelings and thoughts are projections. You are the movie screen on which they play. While the screen never changes, the images change constantly, and the movie itself changes all the time, too. When an angry thought or feeling shows up on the screen, wait. It will morph soon. The screen doesn't fight or resist the projections. It merely provides the space for the movie to play out and waits for it to end.

We talked earlier about the metaphor of the chessboard. You are the board upon which the pieces move and the game is played. Each game has its own character and strategy, but the board never changes. One board might host a thousand struggles; one board might hold the moving pieces (thoughts and feelings) of a lifetime's challenges. But let us be clear: the board is not the game. You are not your thoughts or your feelings.

Let's review a moment: your core self, the piece of you that observes every moment of your life, stands apart from all your thoughts and feelings. The same is true for each of your actions. The observing self watches everything you do but is not your behavior. In particular, your observing self is not your anger-driven actions—it's not the yelling, the name-calling, the hissed threats.

## Fusion

So if the thoughts, feelings, actions, and your observing self are all quite separate, how come they all seem fused in an angry explosion? The reason is that emotions can drive—very quickly—a patterned set of thoughts and habitual behaviors. And for a few moments, we feel taken over by them. It's as if our observing self went off on holiday, leaving our life in the hands of some angry wacko who goes raging around and makes a mess of things.

This apparent fusion of feelings, thoughts, actions, and self is an illusion that our mind creates. It's time now to pull each element apart so your observing self can watch—with mindful acceptance—your anger experience as it really is.

## WISE MIND: SEPARATING THE PIECES OF EXPERIENCE

To get a clearer idea of how to separate the pieces of your experience, let's look at Lacy's story. She's the costume designer for a regional theater and frequently gets upset by actors' demands that she change their costumes at the last minute.

When first asked to explain the anger, Lacy saw no separation between herself and any of her thoughts, feelings, or actions. It was all crushed together in one upsetting experience. Here's how it looked in a diagram. Notice all the circles are overlapping.

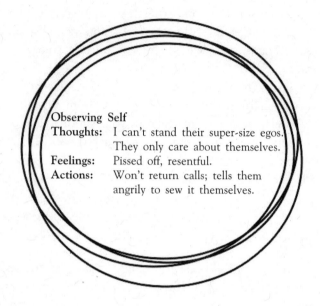

Observing Self
Thoughts:    I can't stand their super-size egos.
             They only care about themselves.
Feelings:    Pissed off, resentful.
Actions:     Won't return calls; tells them
             angrily to sew it themselves.

Lacy's therapist asked her to do a wise mind exercise. She was encouraged to take slow, deep breaths while focusing her attention on her diaphragm. Then the therapist drew a circle and wrote "Observing Self" inside. Below it he drew a row of three more circles. In the first he wrote "Thoughts," in the second, "Feelings," and in the third, "Actions."

"Keep your attention just below your breath," he told Lacy. "This is the place we call wise mind. It's where you can see yourself, watch what's really going on. Now, with your wise, observing mind, fill in the other circles."

Here's what the exercise looked like when Lacy completed it. As you can see, the four circles aren't overlapping anymore. Thoughts, feelings, and actions are now separate and yet connected to and in touch with the observer self.

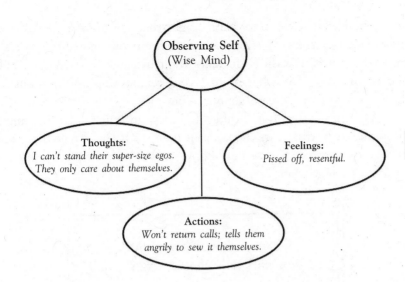

Right now, we'd like you to do the wise mind exercise with a recent anger experience. Breathe deeply, focusing on your diaphragm. Wait until you feel centered. Then visualize the anger scene. From the position of wise mind, observe each element of the experience. Separate your thoughts, feelings, and actions. Now, as Lacy did, write down what you've observed in the diagram below.

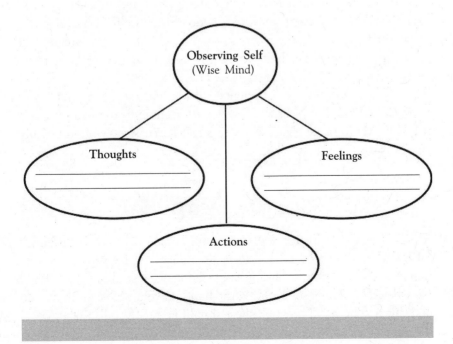

There's one more important insight that can grow from the wise mind exercise: Your behavior is separate from your thoughts and feelings. You can be awash with angry thoughts and emotions and still choose to *act* in ways that protect your relationships. Your thoughts and feelings do not create actions. You do!

The most important thing to keep in mind is this simple awareness: you truly can choose your actions. If you forget that your behavior is a choice, you're not likely to exercise it. So here's a mantra to live by when you're angry:

> *I can't choose how I feel.*
> *I can and will choose what I do.*

## Learning Mindful Acceptance

Now comes the most important part: discovering how to move toward mindful acceptance in your own life. We recommend five key exercises that can teach you how to do this. Mindful breathing will start you focusing on the present moment. Leaves on a stream and journaling the now will both teach you how to notice without resistance each part of your experience. The inner and outer shuttle will help you see and accept experiences inside and outside your body—both pleasant and unpleasant. Finally, a softening to the pain exercise will help you to make peace with pre-anger feelings you've traditionally tried to avoid.

## MINDFUL BREATHING

The best way to start developing mindful acceptance is to learn mindful breathing. Start by taking deep, diaphragmatic breaths. Place one hand on your chest and one on your abdomen, just above your waist. Now begin breathing so that only the hand on your abdomen moves up and down. The hand on your chest should be nearly still. Keep directing your breath downward to the very bottom of your lungs. If it's hard to get the hand on your abdomen to move, press in with that hand. Create pressure on your abdomen, then try to breathe so you push that hand out.

After you've practiced diaphragmatic breathing for a while and you feel like you're getting it, move on to step two: becoming mindful of your breath. Notice the feeling of the cool air as it rushes through your nose, then down the back of your throat. Feel your lungs expanding, experience what it's like as your diaphragm stretches. Make yourself aware of every sensation, every nuance of your breathing.

Good. Now add one more thing: a thought. On the in breath say to yourself: "Live this moment." On the out breath say, "Accept this moment." That's it: breathe deeply, observe your breath, say your mantra.

Practice this exercise twice a day for at least a week. Get good at it. Notice what it teaches you.

## LEAVES ON A STREAM

For this exercise, you again begin with deep, diaphragmatic breathing. After a little while start noticing and labeling each experience that comes up—thoughts, feelings, sensations, and desires or impulses. Pay attention to what's happening in your mind and body, then simply name what's going on. A pain in your foot is a sensation, a judgment about your friend's too-expensive car is a thought, a moment of irritation at struggling with the exercise is a feeling. A sudden yearning to quit and watch some television is an impulse.

Okay. You're watching and labeling each experience as it comes up. Now do one more thing: Imagine sitting next to a stream. As you gaze at the stream you notice a number of large brown autumn leaves on the surface of the water, drifting along in the current.

Now when a thought, a feeling, a sensation, or an impulse comes along into your mind, put it on a leaf. Observe the leaf as it comes closer to you, and then watch as it slowly moves away from you, eventually drifting out of sight. Place each thought, each feeling, each sensation or impulse on its own large leaf and let them just float away downstream.

You can also allow yourself to take the perspective of the stream, just like in the chessboard exercise. Being the stream, you hold each of the leaves and notice the thought or feeling or urge that each leaf carries as it sails by. You need not interfere with them—just let them float by and do what they do until they are eventually carried out of sight.

This exercise helps you practice observing and accepting each experience, then letting go of it. Do this exercise once each day for a week. Notice how you can learn to be an observer rather than a participant or player with a stake in the game.

## JOURNALING THE NOW

This exercise is an extension of the previous leaves on a stream exercise. This time, instead of labeling each experience and visualizing it drifting away, we'd like you to journal the process in a narrative fashion. Use the new language habits we introduced in the previous chapter to help you disentangle yourself from the content of what you experience. Instead of writing "I am sad about losing my friend" write "I'm having the feeling of sadness about losing my friend." When you write "I am sad," you and sadness are one and the same—you and sadness are in overlapping circles. The truth is that you and sadness are not the same. Being sad is just one part of your experience. So is being angry. Here's an example of a narrative:

> *Now I'm having the feeling of a slight headache or pressure behind my eyes. Now I'm having the thought that the back stairs need painting. Now I'm having an impulse to get up and stretch. Now I'm having a thought about how horrible my handwriting is. Now I'm having the feeling of disappointment that the 49ers keep losing. Now I'm having the thought that the owner is an idiot. Now I'm having the feeling of tightness—maybe hunger—in my stomach. Now I'm having thoughts about dinner, starting to want food.*

Notice how the narrative careens from impulse to thought to feeling, and so on. That's how the eternal present really is, if we pay attention. It's just one thing after another, sometimes jumping suddenly without rhyme or reason. Writing it down helps you appreciate and accept the things that occupy your mind.

Keep journaling the now for about three minutes. Don't worry if everything's happening too fast and you don't have time to write an experience down. Just skip it and journal the next thing that comes up.

## INNER AND OUTER SHUTTLE

This mindfulness exercise will help you recognize and appreciate the difference between internal bodily sensations and external sensory experience. What you do is shuttle your awareness back and forth between sensations going on inside your body and sensory experiences coming from outside. Start your focus on one internal bodily sensation (how your stomach, your shoulders, or your aching feet feel). Then immediately switch to an outer experience (the light coming through the window, kids screaming in the next room, or the texture of your armchair upholstery). Now, for three minutes, keep shuttling back and forth—inner, outer, inner, outer.

There's one more part to this exercise. You may notice that some of your inner or outer experiences are uncomfortable. The room's too cold, there's a noise that's bothering you, or something hurts in your body. Good. Every time you notice something uncomfortable, take a deep, diaphragmatic breath and acknowledge the experience. Let the sensation be what it is. Don't fight it. Recognize it for what it is—just a sensation—nothing more, nothing less. Then, in a moment, let your attention shift to the next particle of awareness.

We encourage you to do the shuttle exercise once a day for a week to maximize your benefits from it.

## SOFTENING TO THE PAIN

Now that you've been practicing mindful acceptance of uncomfortable feelings, it's time for the final challenge. For this exercise, you'll visualize a recent anger experience. Rather than just remembering it, see if you can get back to the pre-anger feelings—the hurt, shame, fear, or guilt. Visualize exactly what happened that triggered those feelings. In every way you can, replay the events in your mind until the hurt or shame feels real right now. Take your time. Linger over the details of the scene.

Here comes the most important part: Stay with this painful feeling and start your deep, diaphragmatic breathing. Begin mindful breathing. Let your body soften around the painful feeling. Keep breathing; keep focusing on what it really feels like to breathe in and out—and stay with the experience. See whether you can let go of the anger by softening to and staying with the pain in this moment. After three minutes, shift your attention to something else and end the exercise.

Softening to the pain is a crucial skill, because it will teach you how to stop resisting feelings—even very uncomfortable ones. We know this is a hard skill to learn. So we will work on developing it further in chapter 9. In the meantime, practice softening to the pain every time you have an uncomfortable physical or emotional experience.

### Your Daily Practice

The five exercises you've just learned can be condensed into a brief daily practice. We suggest that you do it for ten minutes at a set time each day. You could tie it to something you always do, such as your morning shower, a meal, arriving home after work, and so on.

Here's the process: Begin by focusing your attention on slow, dia-phragmatic breaths. With each in breath, say to yourself, "Live this moment." On the out breath, say, "Accept this moment." Notice any judgment or fear thoughts. One by one, watch each thought arrive and then drift away. Now notice your experience—what you see and hear, what you feel inside your body. Next, notice your emotions. Be aware of any unpleasant or painful emotions—the ones you don't like or want. Soften to them by breathing mindfully, and accepting whatever you feel.

For ten minutes, keep breathing deeply, keep watching your thoughts, keep softening to and breathing with any discomfort, and stay with the experience. That's it. This daily practice grows more powerful over time. It makes it possible to watch your thoughts and feelings like horses on a merry-go-ground without having to ride them in an endless anger cycle. Get in the habit of relaxing with your pain as you allow it to be what it is, watching it from the distance and safety of your observer self. This practice prepares you to face life's pain and disappointments while finding new ways to respond. When you no longer fight the pain you don't want, the pain loses its grip on you.

# MINDFULNESS WHEN YOU'RE ANGRY: STOP, LOOK, AND LISTEN

The previous exercises are intended for practicing *before* you get angry. Below are two ways to use mindfulness *after* you've gotten angry. They are a bit like the saying "Stop, look, and listen . . . or you won't see what you're missin,'" which your parents may have repeated to you every time you were about to cross the street as a young child.

The first tool, watching the flags, is a process for stopping and noticing the red flags that show up as you're starting to get angry. The goal is to acknowledge these red flags and stay with them without inflaming them or acting on them with anger behavior. The second tool, watching your mouth, is designed to make you stop, look, and listen in on your verbal behavior when you're angry. Chapters 9 and 10 contain additional exercises and suggestions about how you can practice mindful acceptance *after* you've gotten angry.

## Watching the Flags

As soon as something occurs that you didn't expect or want—whether it's an event, in a conversation, or the fact of something *not* happening—stop what you're doing and start watching the flags. These are the red flags signaling that you're starting to get angry: feeling hot, clenching your jaw, throbbing temples, tight stomach, pointing your finger, making fists, voice getting high or loud, heart pounding, feeling shaky, shortness of breath, and so on.

You watch the flags by looking with mindful awareness at what's happening with your body (muscles, breath, heart, temperature), your posture, and your voice. Make no attempt to suppress, reduce, or change the sensations. Just ride them out as in the wave exercise described in chapter 6. Stay firmly in your observer self position for as long as the problematic conversation or situation continues.

## Watching Your Mouth

Once you become aware of feeling angry and you're in a situation with other people, switch your focus to your words—both planned and uttered. Stop and listen to the words in your head before they take shape in your mouth. What is your anger pushing you to say?

If you're in a social situation and it's okay to do so, just be quiet and say nothing. In fact, if it's socially appropriate, leave the situation so you can be alone and stay with your surging anger. It's best not to talk to anyone for as long as you're angry. The reason is that it's virtually impossible not to sound angry when you are angry and feel like you're sitting on a vibrating keg of dynamite. Even saying something like "I love you" may come out sounding more aggressive than kind. Saying nothing or leaving the situation doesn't mean suppressing anger or running away from it. Quite the opposite: you're actually staying with and attending to your anger. That takes more courage and is much harder to do than to speak out in anger.

If you're expected to say something or if it's socially inappropriate to leave the situation, say as little as possible. Listen to each sentence as you start to say it. Each spoken word is a choice you have that can promote harmony or discord, prevent wounds or make them, solve problems or deepen them.

As in the previous exercise, don't try to suppress thoughts and sensations; just notice and acknowledge them. Watching your mouth allows mindful observance of everything your mouth does, or is about to do. It's your key to changing an important part of angry behavior.

Changing anything requires intention. You have to *decide* to do something new. Watching the flags and watching your mouth will only happen with intention. Right now, you can make a commitment to yourself to use these mindfulness techniques whenever something happens that frustrates or disappoints you. Promise yourself that you'll continue practicing mindfulness, as best as you can, until the situation is over.

# THE TAKE-HOME MESSAGE

The five mindful acceptance exercises described in this chapter are building blocks to a critical new skill: embracing what you feel right now without running away from or blocking it. It's important to go beyond reading these exercises. You need to do them. Acceptance takes work and practice. But—and this is a guarantee from us to you—it will change your life.

# WEEK 7
## Learning how to accept what I experience

**Point to ponder:** I can learn to watch the struggle, feel the pain, and honor my hurt with mindful acceptance.

**Questions to consider:** Am I ready to separate my thoughts and feelings from my actions so I can make better choices about what to do when I feel anger? Am I willing to practice mindful acceptance so I can learn to respond to anger in a different way?

# Chapter 8

# Taking Control
of Your Life

*Life is a choice. Psychological pain is not a choice.*
*Either way you go, you will have problems and pain.*
*So the choice here is not about whether or not to have pain.*
*Your choice is whether or not to live a meaningful life.*

—Steven C. Hayes

In previous chapters, we have talked a lot about what you cannot control. The remaining chapters are about what you can control. They are about discovering or perhaps rediscovering what is important to you. You can take charge of and reclaim your life.

# STOP FEEDING THE ANGER TIGER

We often compare anger to a tiger growing inside a person. It starts out like a baby tiger. Each time you act on your anger feeling, you feed the tiger and he gets just a little bit bigger. In the short term, it may not seem this way. But, in the long run, this is what acting on anger does—it feeds your anger, and it cripples your life.

We talked to one of our clients, Frank, a thirty-four year-old store manager, about the anger tiger and asked him to write down his experience. Frank gave us permission to share his therapy journal entry with our readers.

## *Frank's Story*

When this anger tiger first appeared, he was just a baby. In fact, I was just a child back then, too. But it was nasty enough that I wanted it to just go away. Sometimes I got so enraged that I would hit even my best friends. That got me into all sorts of trouble. My anger tiger just kept growing bigger and bigger the more I lashed out at the people who annoyed me. I've been getting more upset all this time because I see the carnage in my life. I feel out of control and like I'm not getting anywhere. The tiger is in charge of my life, and it doesn't look like he's planning on leaving anytime soon. I'm fed up with this and I want to take back my life.

If you're like Frank, the anger tiger has been running your life. The directions you take are chosen not by your highest values, but rather by who or what has pissed you off. Now is the time to ask a critical question: "Who is in control here? Who is choosing? Is it me, or is it the anger tiger?" You don't have to devote your life to feeding the anger tiger. You have the power to choose a different direction.

## LIFE WITHOUT ACTING ON ANGER

Have you ever wondered what your life would be like if you weren't always struggling against anger and rage? Sit back for a moment and think about what kind of things you'd do if your time was no longer consumed by acting on your anger, going after everyone who upsets you, and trying to win the endless battle against the people who are seemingly out to get you and have wronged you. How would you spend your day differently? And how might your relationships be different then?

Now just pause for a moment. Go ahead and sit back, close your eyes, and imagine your new life for a minute or so. Then come back to reading.

We suspect that some of the images that came up in your mind had to do with important aspects of your life that you're missing out on, or may have even given up on, because of anger. We'd like to reconnect you with some of those important parts of your life, because we know that you can reclaim them.

## WHAT ARE MY VALUES?

To figure out what your values are, you'll need to think about areas of your life that are deeply important to you. These are the things that make your life worth living, that you want to cherish and nurture, and that you'd act to defend when necessary. These are the very things that you might look back on at the end of your life and say—if you took good care of them—"There was a life lived well." What you value and consider important may not be exactly what others value and consider important. This is fine and to be expected.

Values tend to fall within several core areas or domains: family, intimate relationships, friends, work, education, leisure, spirituality, citizenship, and health. Although we list them separately, most domains overlap. For example, the value of health can lead you to join a yoga group or sports club. Doing this can in turn lead to meeting new people and being a good friend to people in your life (another value), and being around long enough to be a good parent to your children and grandparent to your grandchildren (another value).

Anger has a way of pushing values from view. If values are at the core of the life you want to lead, then anything—including anger—that gets in the way of your values is a problem.

## Values Are Like a Road Map

Values serve as a map that guides the direction you want to move in. Without values, you are directionless. Anything that hides your values from view can keep you stuck, not knowing where to go. You can end up spinning your wheels through life, feeling like you're getting nowhere fast. You've probably felt this way at some point when you've been angry.

We want to help you stop spinning and get moving in directions that are important to you. Values are the compass that will help guide you away from anger behavior and back into your life. This is the real prize and why it is important for you to reconnect with your values. When you start connecting with what matters in your life, you will want more of your life to focus on that. Once those value-guided directions are clearer to you, you can begin to focus your efforts on moving in those directions.

## Values Help You Stay Focused

Working toward living consistently with what you value will also motivate you to keep up with the exercises in this book. We realize this is not easy and requires commitment. But the investment you make in reading and working with this book will pay off. As you start spending more of your time living consistently with what you value, your life and everything you want to be about will come into focus.

People who have problems with anger often have quite a lot of energy. This energy is a gift. In fact, you can think of your energy as being like a hammer. You can use a hammer to destroy things or to build things. You can likewise focus your energy constructively or destructively in your life, whether that means getting even or being a loving partner, a good friend, an athlete, or whatever else you desire. As you explore your valued directions in this chapter, keep thinking about this question: "How can I use my energy wisely?"

## Values Give You an Alternative to Blowing Up in Anger

Values serve as a benchmark to evaluate which actions are useful and which aren't. This is especially important when you feel angry and wonder what to do about it. Values guide you toward actions that exemplify what you want your life to be about. You will learn a response to anger feelings that involves stopping, observing, and then considering your values along these lines: "Acting on this anger feeling will probably conflict with one of my values. It will hurt someone I love. It can affect my status at work." You will know what to do and what not to do by answering the following question: "Does this action move me closer to or further away from my values?"

Values are not a distraction from anger. Instead, they help you decide what matters more: getting even or living a life you value. That's how working toward what matters to you becomes a viable alternative to blowing up in anger.

For example, let's say you have chosen being a loving husband as one of your values. One day your wife approaches you. She's upset and demands an answer to her question of why you can't be more understanding about her situation as a working mother. Your values help you ask yourself the following question: "What is moving me closer to being a loving husband: snapping back at her right away and defending myself (that's what I feel like doing), or being quiet for a while, stroking her hand, and admitting with a kind tone of voice that she's in a difficult situation, and telling her that I'll make an effort to help her?"

One of our clients, Jim, would routinely fly off the handle when his daughter didn't clean up her room. He would raise his voice and ultimately say something that left his daughter in tears. He would usually walk away fuming. The last time this began to unfold, Jim took stock of what he cared about—his relationship with his daughter. This time, he didn't flare up and instead approached his daughter, hugged her, and said that he cared about her and loved her. When he committed to this way of interacting with his daughter, their relationship improved and she made an effort to keep her room clean because she wanted to please him.

A life lived in the service of anger is typically not high on anyone's list of values. Jim came to this realization, too, as he put his value of a good relationship with his daughter into clear focus.

You're at a critical choice point in your life. You can choose to live it in a way that upholds your deepest and most cherished desires, or you can choose the same old way of life ruled by anger. It's up to you.

You can think of these choices in this way: Imagine life as a walk down a long corridor with many doors on either side. You have the power to choose which doors to open and enter. One of those doors is labeled "anger." You have chosen the anger behavior door for so long that you may have lost sight of other options in the corridor. You can venture out and open up other doors. You can also choose to stay inside the anger room.

What choice do you want to make? Staying locked behind the anger door limits your life. Anger pushes away the family members you love and moves you further away from having a satisfying family life. Anger also pushes away friends who are concerned about you or could help you. Now is the time to muster the courage to explore other doors in your life corridor. Think about your life. Besides anger, what other doors can you and would you like to open? Maybe there's a door labeled "love" and another sporting a sign that says "physical fitness." There's a door to professional satisfaction, and another that leads to political activism. Yet another is marked "inner peace." It's a long corridor with many, many doors.

## IS IT A GOAL OR A VALUE?

It's easy to confuse goals with values. Goals are actions you can put on a list, complete, and then check off. Once you reach a goal, the work is done, and you're finished. Taking out the garbage is a goal you can check off, as are other goals such as losing ten pounds, taking a vacation, getting a degree, or mowing the lawn. Even the act of getting married fits our definition of a goal. Once that ring is on your finger, your goal is achieved. So, you can tell if something is a goal by whether you can do it and then get it off your plate.

Unlike goals, values are lifelong journeys. You can't answer the question "Am I done yet?" with values. Values have no end point. Instead, they direct us throughout life.

For example, reaching a particular goal (getting married) is just one of many steps in a valued direction (being a loving partner). The value of being a loving, devoted partner is not complete the moment you say, "I do." Being a loving, devoted partner is something you must constantly keep on working toward, and there is always room for growth. Likewise, reaching your goal of spending two hours of quality time with your child every weekend does not complete the value of being a good parent. Values such as being a loving person or a good parent are ongoing commitments and actions you cannot finish while you're alive.

Although values and goals are not the same, they are related. Just think of one or two goals you have set for yourself. Be open to the seemingly mundane here too, like taking out the garbage to please your wife. To determine the value that underlies the goal, you can simply ask yourself, "Why am I doing this?" "What am I trying to accomplish in my life with this goal?" "Where am I heading with this?" Answers to these questions will point you in the direction of your values. You may find the simple act of taking out the garbage reflects a value of helping, being part of a family, or being a supportive spouse.

## Outcomes

Sometimes we hear people say, "I want to be calmer," or "It's important for me to be happy." Both statements sound like values, but they are really goals. Being calmer and happier are emotional goals. Essentially, they are an outcome, a result that may or may not happen after you start moving toward your values. Remember, values are a direction that must be lived out again and again by actions, large and small, each and every day. In a nutshell, values are the cumulative effect of what you spend your time doing, not what you think and feel about what you're doing.

## If a Dead Man Can Do It, It's Not a Good Goal

As you think about values, think about what you want to or can do, not what you don't want to do or can't do. Examples of to-do goals include call my best friend at least once a week, enrol in a music class, attend church once a week, exercise thirty minutes daily, read to my children every night before bed, and so on.

Many of us have a tendency to focus our time and effort on not-to-do goals. These not-to-dos often show up after you've done something hurtful, and when you let your feelings and thoughts guide your actions. Sara found herself doing quite a bit of this. She would frequently spend her time telling herself "Don't yell at the kids," "Stop criticizing Dan [her husband]," or "Don't get worked up when others are late."

Anytime you write or think "don't," "never," "stop," "quit," and the like, you are setting what we call a dead man's goal. Dead men don't yell at their children or criticize their spouse. If you start to write a dead man's goal, ask yourself, "What can I *do* instead?" This simple question helps reframe your not-to-do into a to-do. When you know what to do, you have a direction and can start doing. So, instead of saying "Stop criticizing my partner," you might instead focus on behaving in a more loving, compassionate fashion toward your partner by doing things that show you care. When you only know what not to do, you are as exiled from life as a dead man.

### Valuing Involves Action, Not Feeling

Many people assume that valuing is how they *feel* about a particular area in their lives. This is a potential trap. There are many actions you take in life regardless of how you may feel at the time. You probably go to work in the morning regardless of whether you feel irritated, sad, anxious, or happy. Or you may have paid a visit to Aunt Edith even if you don't like her much. So, if you feel angry at someone you love, you can still reach out to them and give them a hug or a gift even though inside you feel resentful. This is why we stress that valuing is all about action. You actually value with your hands, feet, and words. If you say you value your career, then you should be doing just that: working to build your career. If you don't work to build your career, then you don't value it, regardless of how you *feel* about it.

# WHAT DO YOU WANT YOUR LIFE TO STAND FOR?

Have you ever thought about what you want your life to stand for? Most people don't think about this until it's too late to do something about it. To help you avoid this sad outcome, we're going to walk you through two exercises: a funeral meditation and writing your own epitaph. These exercises are very powerful, perhaps even a little frightening. The payoff for doing them is that they will give you a clear vision of what you want your life to stand for, and they'll begin to reveal what you truly value in your life.

Death is inevitable. We can delay death, but we can never avoid it. Although you can't control when or how you will die, you can control how you live. The following exercise will help you make contact with this simple truism in a profound way.

## FUNERAL MEDITATION

Go ahead and get comfortable. For this exercise, imagine that you're watching your own funeral. Visualize yourself in an open casket. Smell the fresh flowers. Hear the soft music in the background. Look around the room. Who do you see? Perhaps you can see your loved ones, family, friends, relatives, coworkers, and acquaintances. Listen closely to their conversations; eavesdrop on what they are saying about you. What is your partner saying . . . your kids . . . your best friend . . . your colleagues . . . your neighbor?

Listen carefully to each of them as they say the words that, in your heart, you most want to hear about yourself. This is how you want the people whom you care about to remember you. Your wisdom will let you pick and choose exactly what you want and need to hear from them.

Pause for a moment and continue to imagine this situation. Stay with this image for a few minutes. Then come back to reading.

Think about the comments you heard that touched and pleased you. These will give you an idea of what you really want your life to be about. Some of what you heard may have left you feeling hurt and disappointed. Perhaps one person said, "He was a cynical, angry man," or "She was often quite bitchy." The good news about this exercise is that your life isn't over yet, and the private conversations at your funeral have not yet taken place. You still have time to do things so that you will be sorely missed and remembered as the type of person you want to be. You can start living that way right now.

## WRITE YOUR OWN EPITAPH

Imagine that one day the headstone in the drawing below will be the headstone on your grave. Notice that the headstone is blank. Your epitaph (a brief description of your life) has not yet been written. What inscription would you like to see on your headstone? Think of a phrase or sentence that would capture the essence of the life you want to have led. What is it you want to be remembered for? Give yourself some time to think about these important questions. If you find an answer—or more than one—write them down on the headstone. This may seem like another strange and somewhat scary exercise. However, if you stick with it and complete it—even if you feel a bit queasy—it will help you get in touch with what you really want your life to stand for.

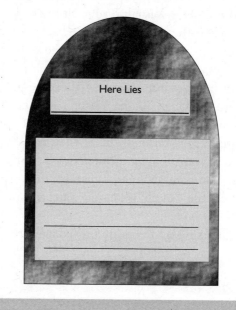

This is not really a hypothetical exercise. What you will be remembered for, what defines your life, is up to you. It depends on what you do now. It depends on the actions you take being consistent with what you care about. This is one way you can help determine the wording of your own epitaph.

Now, we make no promises that people will build a Lincoln-type memorial for you at the end of your life. Yet if you make positive steps to take your life in the direction of your values, chances are that you'll be remembered with warmth and love by all who know you.

Living your values is a lifelong journey. Each day you live is a day an opportunity to move in a valued direction while taking your painful thoughts and feelings with you. You write your own eulogy and epitaph by the choices you make and the actions you take each and every day. So what do you want your epitaph to say? What sorts of things do you want to have people murmuring at your memorial? Answering these questions will point you in the direction you want to go.

## IDENTIFYING VALUED LIFE DIRECTIONS— THE LIFE COMPASS

Identifying your values and setting goals are important steps on the road to living the life you want to lead. To identify your core values, you can ask yourself a couple of simple questions: "What do I want my life to be about?" "What really matters to me?" To get to the heart of such questions, we encourage you to complete the life compass. It will take a while to complete, but it's time well spent because it will help you figure out some important things:

- Which areas of your life are most important to you

- How you would like to conduct your life vis-à-vis the things that matter most

- How consistent your actions have been with your intentions

- Obstacles or barriers that stand in the way of pursuing your values

### What Life Domains Do You Value and Find Important?

Take a look at figure 2 so you'll have some context for this exercise. The first step in this exercise is to consider your quality of life in each of the ten life domain areas. One aspect of quality of life involves the emphasis you put on each of these ten areas. Start by rating the importance of each area using a scale of 0 (unimportant), 1 (moderately important), or 2 (very important). Write your importance ratings into the "i" box connected to each value. Not everyone will value all of these areas, or value all areas the same. Rate each area according to your own personal sense of importance. Go ahead and do this now.

## What Are Your Intentions?

Next, go back to each area you rated as either moderately important (1), or very important (2), and write down your intention. Your intention is simply a statement of how you would like to live your life in that area (for example, what is most important to you in that area?). Write that intention directly in the box. If you're having difficulty coming up with an intention statement because you're unsure what a particular domain is about, you can ask yourself the following questions:

- **Intimate relationships:** What kind of partner would I most like to be in an intimate relationship? What type of marital or couple relationship would I like to have? How do I want to treat my partner?

- **Parenting:** What type of parent do I want to be? How do I want to interact with my children?

- **Education/learning:** Why is learning important to me? What skills, training, or areas of competence would I like to acquire?

- **Friends/social life:** What kind of friend do I want to be? What does it mean to be a good friend? How do I behave toward my best friend? Why is friendship important to me?

- **Physical self-care/health:** How and why do I take care of myself? Why do I want to take care of my body and my health through what I eat, by exercising, and by being physically fit?

- **Family of origin:** How do I want to interact with my family members? What type of sister or brother do I want to be? What type of son or daughter do I want to be?

- **Spirituality:** What are the mysteries of life before which I stand in awe? What are the things larger than my own life that inspire me? In what (if anything) do I have faith?

■ **Community life/citizenship:** What can I do to make the world a better place? Why are community activities (such as volunteering, voting, recycling) important to me?

■ **Recreation/leisure:** How do I feed myself through hobbies, sports, or play? Why do I enjoy them?

■ **Work/career:** What do I want my work or career to be about or stand for? What is important to me about my work (for example, financial security, intellectual challenge, independence, prestige, or interacting with or helping people)?

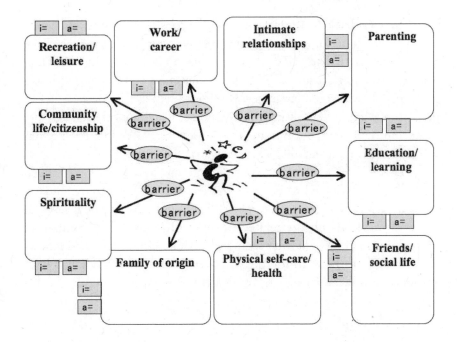

Figure 2. The Life Compass—a behavioral compass of important life domains, intentions in each area, and potential barriers to reaching those goals (adapted from Dahl et al., 2004; Copyright (2004) by the Association for Advancement of Behavior Therapy. Reprinted by permission of the publisher.

## Are You Doing What Matters to You?

After you've finished writing down your intentions on the life compass, please think about your activities in the past week. How consistent have your actions been with your intentions in each area? If we call your activities "your feet," how consistent were your feet with the intentions you just wrote down? For each intention, rate how often you have done something to move you forward in this area during the past seven days. Use the following scale for your ratings: 0 = no action, 1 = one or two activities or actions, 2 = three or four activities, 3 = five or more activities. Write your ratings in the "a" = (actions) box next to the "i" box connected to each value. We're not asking about your ideal in each area or what others may think of you. Just rate how actively you have you been working toward your intentions during the past week.

## What Stands in Your Way?

Now go back and look at your intentions and actions. How well do they match up for each domain you rated as important to you? Take stock here, particularly of areas where the "i" is a larger number than the "a." Are you doing things that are important to you? If you're like most people with problem anger, you might see discrepancies between importance and action ratings. For instance, if you consider family very important and your action rating is low (0 or 1), you're living a life that is quite different from the one you want.

Discrepancies between your intentions and actions in valued areas are often related to barriers. Barriers are anything that stands in the way of you living out your values. If you look deeply, you'll see that some of these are directly related to your hurt and anger. The flash of anger can sidetrack you from seeing your valued intentions and following through on them. In the next two chapters, we'll provide you with some skills to identify and overcome these barriers.

# THE TAKE-HOME MESSAGE

You can take charge of your life by focusing on what you can control: what you do with your hands, feet, and mouth. Instead of giving in to anger feelings, you can identify what truly matters in your life and then focus your energy on pursuing goals that will move you in those directions.

The values you choose are the road map for guiding you in the process of reclaiming your life from anger. They help you stay focused on what matters. When you feel the anger sensations surging in your body, you can stop, observe the feeling, and then listen to your values. They will help you choose a course of action that moves you closer to rather than away from your value-driven goals. This is how living for your values can become an alternative to blowing up in anger.

Pursuing your values is all about action. You can write your own eulogy and epitaph through the choices you make and the actions you take every day. Each day you live is a day to move in a valued direction *and* take your painful thoughts and feelings with you.

---

### WEEK 8
#### Identifying and thinking about my values

**Point to ponder:** Life is short. My values make my life worthwhile.

**Questions to consider:** Am I living consistently with my values, or am I letting my anger and emotional pain get in the way of my values? Am I ready to start moving in the direction of my values and take anger, hurt, *and* joy along for the ride?

# Chapter 9

# Facing the Flame of Anger and the Pain Fueling It

*Of the Seven Deadly Sins, anger is possibly the most fun. To lick your wounds, to smack your lips over grievances long past, to roll over your tongue the prospect of bitter confrontations still to come, to savor to the last toothsome morsel both the pain you are given and the pain you are giving back—in many ways it is a feast fit for a king. The chief drawback is that what you are wolfing down is yourself. The skeleton at the feast is you.*

—Frederick Buechner

Unforgiveness is the seed of resentment and bitterness. It's the key ingredient in the feast of anger that transforms emotional pain and hurt into suffering and misery. Like a cancer, unforgiveness allows anger to grow and your heart to harden, while breeding judgment, criticism, blame, ill will, and a host of harmful behavioral tendencies.

When people fail you in some way, the natural tendency is to feel hurt, used, robbed, or wronged—like they owe you. This is what you get when you don't forgive—an ever-present debt to be repaid, with you stuck as the victim. This is why forgiveness is vital. "Forgiveness" means "for giving," the release of an imagined debt: softening up to the pain and hurt you experience, giving it loving compassion and acceptance, and then letting it go. When you choose forgiveness, you cut out anger at its root and allow peace to settle in.

Patience is about getting smart and just stopping, sitting still, and waiting when the hardness of the hot, noisy, pulsating, wanting-to-just-get-even state of mind shows up. You can make a decision to cultivate patience in your life by learning to sit still with your pain, hurt, and resentment—and do nothing. This simple and yet difficult move will help you take your life in directions you want it to go.

Forgiveness and patience are the most powerful antidotes to anger and aggression. And neither comes easy. Building on previous exercises, we'll offer you more ways to nurture and develop your capacity for forgiveness and patience. We'll teach you how to forgive yourself and others, take care of your pain and hurt, and practice patience to cool the flames of anger when they flare up.

Pema Chödrön (2001, 2005) has written widely about the wisdom of approaching anger with mindful acceptance and compassion, and practicing patience with anger. We have included many of her suggestions in the exercises in this and the next chapter. It's best to practice patience at home first, so that you can apply this vital life skill later in those critical stressful situations when painful emotions run high.

---

# LEARNING TO FORGIVE

Most major religions tell us that forgiveness is good, but they do not teach us how to go about doing it. Many studies report that the ability to forgive improves health—physical, emotional and spiritual (McCullough, Thoresen, and Pargament 2000). Studies also show that you can learn to forgive. Those who learn this important skill report experiencing less hurt, stress, anger, depression, and illness, and more energy, hope, optimism, compassion, and love, and a greater sense of well-being. These are some of the concrete benefits of forgiveness.

Just as with acceptance, many people think forgiving means condoning or forgetting past wrongs, ignoring hurt and pain; or else they see it as a sign of weakness. None of this is true. When the late Pope John Paul II met with his would-be assassin to forgive him, he wasn't condoning the wrong that was done. Instead, he was extending mercy and compassion. He was letting go. The man who tried to kill the Pope still sits in prison for his crime.

It is much easier to be angry than to choose forgiveness. Forgiving is the most courageous and beneficial thing you can do for yourself. It's a gift to yourself. To experience the benefits of forgiveness, you need no other person than yourself.

## Four Steps to Forgiveness

Below we describe an exercise that outlines four steps on the path to learning forgiveness:

1. **Awareness:** Waking up to your hurt and pain as it is, without judgment or denial

2. **Separation:** Softening to your experience using your wise mind while inviting healing and change

3. **Compassionate witness:** Extending compassion to your experience and that of others

4. **Letting go and moving on:** Releasing the grudges, resentment, and pain, and then moving forward in your life in directions you want to go

Before beginning this exercise, we'd like you to find a quiet, comfortable place where you can set up a candle. Light this candle as a symbol of your commitment to forgive. This candle represents someone who recently caused you pain or hurt. You will be focusing on the flame as you go through each step.

This exercise is likely to be difficult for you at first. Steps 3 and 4, bringing compassion and letting go as you extend forgiveness to the source of hurt or pain, are particularly tough at first. Be gentle with yourself if it feels like it's too much or too difficult. Your mind will give you all sorts of reasons why you shouldn't do it. Acknowledge those doubts, apprehensions, and uneasiness about extending forgiveness *and* see whether you can be willing to have them for the sake of living the life you want. It takes practice to cultivate forgiveness. Give yourself time to get the hang of it. Spend at least fifteen minutes doing this exercise at least once per day. Tape-record it at a slow pace if that makes it easier for you. Remember, this is for you, not for those who have hurt you!

## THE CANDLE OF FORGIVENESS

Go ahead and light the candle, and then get in a comfortable position in your chair. Sit upright with your feet flat on the floor, your arms and legs uncrossed, and your hands resting in your lap (palms up or down, whichever is more comfortable). Allow your eyes to focus on the candle flame and simply watch it.

As you watch the flicker of the candle flame, bring your attention to the gentle rising and falling of your breath in your chest and belly. Like ocean waves coming in and out, your breath is always there. Notice its rhythm in your body. Notice each breath. Focus on each inhale . . . and exhale. Notice the changing patterns of sensations in your belly as you breathe in, and as you breathe out. Take a few minutes to feel the physical sensations as you inhale and exhale.

### Step 1: Acknowledge the Wrong and Hurt Underneath the Anger

Now allow your awareness to shift to a recent situation where you became angry. See if you can allow yourself to visualize the scene fully. What happened? Who else was there? Watch the candle as you acknowledge the anger situation unfolding in your mind's eye. Focus on your breathing as you watch the situation unfold. With each slow breath, see if you can slow the anger situation down, like a slow-motion movie. As you do, bring your attention to any sensations of discomfort that show up. As best you can, bring an attitude of generous allowing and gentle acceptance to your experience right now. See if you can make room for the pain and hurt you had then and that you may be reliving now. Soften to it . . . as you breathe in . . . and out . . .

in and out. Don't try to fight what you experience. Open up to all of it: the hurt, pain, sadness, regret, loss, and resentment. Allow yourself to become more aware of your hurt and painful emotions, and simply acknowledge the hurt you experienced and the hurt you may have caused. Don't blame. Simply acknowledge and become aware of your experience.

## Step 2: Separate Hurtful Actions from Your Hurt and Its Source

Visualize the person who hurt you. As you begin to visualize that person, allow them to drift over to the candle and become the candle. Focus on the candle as the person who hurt you, and remember what happened. As you focus on the candle, notice what your mind, the language machine, is doing, and the sensations that come up. You might see your mind passing judgment . . . blaming . . . and lingering over feelings of sadness . . . bitterness . . . resentment. As these and other thoughts and sensations come into your awareness, simply label them as you did in previous exercises—"There is judgment . . . blame . . . tension . . . resentment"—and allow them to be. Bring a gentle and kind awareness to your pain and hurt as you breathe in . . . and out . . . in . . . and out . . . slowly, and deeply.

Next, create some space between the actions that made you feel hurt and angry and the person who committed them. If it helps, you can visualize the action that hurt you as the flame and the person who committed the hurt as the candlestick. Notice the difference between the flame and the candle. The flame is not the candlestick. The actions of the person who hurt you are not the same as the person who committed them. As you breathe in and out, give yourself time to connect with this difference. Bring each hurtful action into the flame, one by one, and notice it, label it, and then see the difference between the hurtful action and the person who committed it. Visualize what was done, not who did it.

Then, after you spend some time noticing each action, allow it to disappear up into the heat leaving the candle flame. Keep watching any tension, discomfort, anger, hurt, or whatever else your body may be doing. Make room for what you experience as you return your attention to your body and your breathing. Don't change or fix anything.

## Step 3: Bring Compassionate Witness to Your Hurt

Next, bring your attention back to the human being symbolized by the candle—the perpetrator of wrongs against you. Notice how he or she is also a person who is vulnerable to harm, just like you. At a basic human level, the two of you are not that different. See if you can allow yourself to take his or her perspective as a compassionate witness—see what life might be like through that person's eyes. Connect with his or her hardships, losses, missed opportunities, poor choices, faults and failings, hurts and sadness, hopes and dreams.

Without condoning that person's actions, see if you can connect with his or her humanity and imperfections as you connect with your own humanity and imperfections, hardships, loss, pain, and suffering. As a compassionate witness to this other human being, see if you can connect more deeply with that person as another human being. Notice the offender's thoughts and feelings, knowing that you've also experienced similar types of thoughts and feelings. What might it be like to have lived the life of the person who offended you? As best you can, bring an attitude of generous allowing and gentle acceptance to what you experience now.

## Step 4: Extend Forgiveness, Let Go, and Move On

Now see if you can bring into awareness what your life would be like if you let go of all the negative energy you are holding on to—your grievances, grudges, bitterness, and anger. Connect with the reasons behind why you want to be free from anger and the desire for revenge. Allow yourself to visualize an alternative future full of the things you have missed out on or given up by not offering forgiveness. See if you can connect with your future without amnesia about what has happened in the past, and without carrying the weight of bitterness, anger, and resentment toward the person who hurt you.

Allow yourself to take the courageous step forward in your life of letting go of your anger and resentment. Perhaps you can feel the burden and weight of past hurts and unresolved anger begin to lift from your shoulders. Take time to really connect with this relief as you imagine yourself separating from the resentment and bitterness you have carried for so long. Allow all of it to drift away with each out breath, and with each in breath welcome peace and forgiveness. Continue to breathe in . . . and out. Slowly. Deeply.

When you're ready, bring into your awareness how you have needed other people's forgiveness in the past. Imagine extending that forgiveness to the person who hurt or offended you. What could you say to that person now? As you think about this, notice any discomfort showing up and how your mind is reacting. If the thought "The person doesn't deserve that" shows up, just notice that thought and gently let it go. Return your focus to your breathing as you remind yourself that kind and gentle acts of forgiveness are for *you*, not for others. Imagine the weight of the burden being lifted from you as you choose to give forgiveness. Allow yourself to connect with the sense of healing and control that comes along with this. As you give the powerful gift of forgiveness, notice some budding feelings of softness where before there was only hardness, hurt, and pain.

Embrace this moment of peace as you return to the image of the person who offended you. Gently extend your hands as you say, "In forgiving you, I forgive myself. In letting go of my anger toward you, I bring peace to myself. I invite peace and compassion into my life and into my hurt and pain. I choose to let go of this burden that I have been carrying for so long." Repeat these phrases slowly as you extend forgiveness.

Stay with and simply observe and label whatever thoughts and feelings come up as you extend this act of forgiveness. Sense the emotional relief that comes when the burden of a grudge is melting away. See if you can notice the peace and feeling of inner strength that comes about as you extend compassion and forgiveness in this moment. Then, when you're ready, bring your awareness back into the room, to your body, and to the flicker of the candle flame. Finish this exercise by blowing out the candle as a symbolic gesture of your commitment to forgive and let go, and your readiness to move on with your life.

## Barriers to Forgiveness

A recent Gallup poll showed that 94 percent of Americans believe that it is important to forgive, and yet only 48 percent reported that they routinely practice forgiving others. Something is getting in the way of people offering forgiveness as often as they'd like to. The chief barriers to forgiveness are mental—the same kinds of mind chatter that seem to protect you from hurt and pain but actually help fuel your anger and keep you stuck and hurting. You'll need to face each of these barriers squarely and recognize them for what they are if you want to release yourself from the grip of problem anger.

## Larry's Story

Let's look at how this played out with Larry, who recently attended an anger and forgiveness workshop. About two months before the workshop, Larry learned that his wife of fifteen years had lied to him about something that had a major impact on their future. He had suspected that his wife had lied to him in the past about fairly important financial matters, but now the full extent of her deception was revealed. Even though the revelation came to light two months previously, Larry was still struggling with feelings of hurt and betrayal, and he wanted to learn how to deal with them. His anger and hurt were as vivid as they'd been when he'd first unearthed the lie. Larry loved his wife, but he had qualms about forgiving her. He asked himself these questions:

- If I forgive my wife, am I condoning her deception?

- How can I forget that she blew most of our savings?

- How can I stop obsessing and fuming over this?

Larry learned over the next several weeks a few simple facts: Just because someone hurt you doesn't mean that you have to suffer endlessly. Forgiveness did not mean excusing or glossing over his wife's deception. It did not mean naively trusting her, and it didn't even necessarily mean that they'd stay together. Forgiving simply meant choosing to let go of his resentment. Larry also learned that there is no such thing as trying to forgive. You either forgive or you don't.

## TRYING TO FORGIVE VERSUS FORGIVING

"I'll try" was Larry's first response when asked whether he was willing to forgive his wife and let go of his anger and hurt. Perhaps you've also tried to forgive someone. Maybe you've said something to yourself like "I tried to forgive, but [he or she] doesn't deserve it" or "Why should I forgive what happened when I suffered so much because of it?" Maybe what happened was so horrible that you feel you could not possibly forgive the person who harmed you.

This brief exercise is a powerful way for you to connect with the fact that forgiveness is something you do for yourself—and it's also an all-or-nothing action: You do or you don't; it's not something you try to do.

To get a sense of what we mean, go ahead and have a seat at a table and place a pen in front of you. Now, we would like you to *try* to pick up the pen. Try as hard as you can. Go ahead and *try* it. If you find yourself picking up the pen, stop! That is not what we asked you to do. We want you to *try* to pick it up.

After some effort, you're probably thinking, "Well, I can't do that. Either I pick it up or I don't." You're right. There is no way to try to pick up the pen and at the same time pick it up.

Trying is actually a form of not doing. This is why we never want you to try anything. You must first make a choice about whether you're willing to do something. If you are willing—if you are *completely* willing, rather than just a bit willing—then go ahead and do it. And if you aren't willing, then don't do it.

Doing is not about getting it right or meeting failure. For instance, you could decide to pick up the pen and then find that it slips from your fingers and drops to the floor. Your mind might say, "You tried, but it didn't work." Yet your experience tells you that you could still bend over and repeat the act of picking up the pen, if that's what you're committed to doing. Some activities in life simply require persistence; you may need to do them over and over again before you've accomplished your goal.

Failure is a subjective evaluation by what we like to call your mind machine. Such evaluations need not stop you from doing what is important, even if that doing is a trial-and-error process that is played out over time.

Forgiveness is a process that fits this bill. For Larry, forgiveness was a painful process that led him to confront two critical questions about the usefulness of resentment: First, did being upset and angry for the past eight weeks change what had happened? Second, would choosing to hang on to his resentment in the coming months and years change what had happened? Larry, of course, knew the answers. He loved his wife and family deeply and did not want to ruin the next months and years of his life, marriage, career, and family. So he was willing to forgive and let go. (And he and his wife went into marriage counseling to deal with their communication problems.)

Forgiveness takes hard work and courage, because you need to be willing to confront your pain and hurt with renewed compassion, gentleness, and patience. Larry did this by making space for his hurt and discomfort and by choosing not to buy into his evaluative mind. You can do this, too, by opening up, observing, softening to, and appreciating all of what you experience, both the pleasures and the sorrows, the good times and the difficult times. How you act in all these life situations is up to you: this is something that you can control.

## FACING YOUR ANGER AND HURT

Behind all anger is unresolved and often hidden pain and hurt. The exercises below are designed to bring you into close contact with your hurt and emotional pain. Practice them at home first, so that you can apply the skills later in situations where your anger gets triggered. The long-term goal is to develop a willingness to be in contact with your anger and sit still with it.

When you learn to witness and accept your pain and hurt, you remove the fuel from anger—and you make room for compassion and forgiveness. In the process, you'll learn several new things:

I.  You'll develop greater honesty about your experience. You'll learn to acknowledge anger, rage, fear, guilt, rejection, and hurt when you feel them.

2. You'll develop the courage to do nothing, to just sit with your anger. This part is critical. You'll learn to stop running from yourself, and you'll develop comfort in your own skin. There is simply no way to be compassionate about your experience while you're busy running away from it.

3. You'll develop an observer's perspective on your experience. Watching without judging will allow you to disentangle yourself from what your body and mind are doing. This will give you the control to act in ways that matter to you, rather than reacting without control. It will free you to let go and move forward in your life.

Doing these exercises is likely to be scary at first. But if you stick with them, you will find that your anger is far more harmful and damaging than the hurt and pain beneath. It's the anger that's ruining your life, not your capacity to hurt and feel emotional pain. Wholeheartedly practicing these exercises daily is extremely important to your progress toward getting out of the anger trap and into your life. Do not attempt the exercises if you merely feel like *trying* them. Wait until you're ready to do them, and then find a quiet place and follow through.

The next exercise is one of the most important ones in this book. Set aside ten to fifteen minutes for doing it. As before, with the anger armor exercise, we recommend that you read through the script a few times first. Then close your eyes and follow the instructions. You can also record the script on an audio cassette and play it back to yourself while you practice.

## SITTING WITH YOUR ANGER AND DIVING INTO YOUR HURT

Once again, get in a comfortable position in a chair. Sit upright with your feet flat on the floor, your arms and legs uncrossed, and your hands resting in your lap (palms up or down, whichever is more comfortable). Close your eyes and take a few deep breaths. Relax. Allow your body to rest without drifting off to sleep.

Now bring into your awareness a recent situation where you felt anger. Really work to bring this experience into your full awareness and right into the room with you. Make it as real as possible. Continue to visualize the situation until you can really notice a wave of unpleasant changes sweeping over your body and mind. Allow yourself to connect with the experience. Relive every bit of it as best as you can. Keep doing so until you're at a point where you feel taken over by feelings of anger and a strong desire to do something about it.

Now we want you to go more deeply into this experience. Imagine that you have a large bubble wand like kids sometimes play with at the beach or in the park. Go ahead and fill the wand with soap, getting it ready to form a giant bubble. Then, look within yourself and notice all the elements of the anger experience. Start by locating judgments and blaming thoughts. For each one, take your bubble wand and sweep it through. Trap each thought in a giant bubble. Then, one by one, notice each thought in its bubble. Label each one as you watch it drift upward in the gentle breeze: "There goes judging . . . blaming . . . criticizing." Keep watching as all of them go higher and higher until they're out of sight. Then, take a few slow, deep breaths.

Next, notice the physical sensations of anger in your body: heart pounding in your chest, feeling shaky, trembling hands, shortness of breath, feeling hot, feeling sick to your stomach. There is tension everywhere. You feel like exploding. As you feel impulses to respond, label them one at a time: "There is my impulse to shout . . . make a fist . . . lash out . . . point my finger." Your task now is both simple and difficult: Do nothing! Sit with these sensations and impulses. Feel the restlessness of the energy in this situation. Sitting still and doing nothing is the last thing you want to do, *and* it is the wisest thing you can do. Say nothing. Do nothing. You want resolution now, and there isn't any.

The energy of anger works like the big ocean wave we described in chapter 5. Continue to sit still with the energy you feel in this situation, and let the anger wave run its course. Watch as it crests, staying strong and powerful for a while until it eventually loses force and dissipates.

Now, gently return to the anger situation and take a final inventory. What are you left with? What do you see? We predict that there are only two things left. You still have the pain and hurt that fueled your anger to begin with. And you still have your values—although they might feel a bit bruised and beat up by the anger. First, turn your attention to the pain and hurt. As you did in the anger armor exercise, find a label to identify each feeling. Take a moment to really take stock.

Perhaps you can see hurt, fear, abandonment, loneliness, feelings of inadequacy, loss, guilt, or shame. There is no need to deny or hide these feelings. They are part of you and belong to you, without being you or defining who you are. Just allow them to be, and see if you can make space for them. Treat them like an open wound: take care of them by bringing kindness, care, and compassion to your experience and to this moment. Forgive yourself for burying and rejecting your pain for so long, for acting in ways to push it from view.

If at any time you feel like stopping and stepping back inside the anger armor, thank your mind for that option, and simply return to your experience. If you notice judgment or resentment popping up again, place them into their own bubbles and let them go, floating upward.

Next, gently turn your attention to your values, which are lying close by. Which ones do you see? Pick one or two that are particularly important to you. Now ask yourself this important question: "If anger and hurt stand between me and moving in the direction of those values, am I willing to own them and still do what matters to me?" If you're willing, anger will no longer be a barrier.

Think of a situation where anger has gotten in the way of acting in accordance with your values. Then, go ahead and imagine yourself doing what you value in this situation while bringing your hurt and pain with you. That probably feels strange; and it will also feel vital, because you're moving toward what you care about in life. You're exerting control where you truly have it. Take time to really connect with this concept. Feeling your anger, your hurt, and your pain while acting to promote your values is what it's all about!

Then, when you're ready, gradually widen your attention to take in the sounds around you. Take a moment to resolve to bring a sense of compassion and forgiveness into the present moment and to the rest of your day.

Doing this exercise isn't easy. You may at first have problems taking an observer's perspective and bringing some kindness to this experience. Don't beat yourself up over this; don't judge those difficulties as failures. Compassion doesn't require perfection. Just stay the course, be patient, and relax with yourself. Simply commit to doing the exercise again tomorrow, and again the next day. Do the best you can.

We suggest that you continue to go over the same anger episode once a day until you can more readily adopt a wise mind perspective as you stay with the negative energy and hurt you feel. Then, move on to different anger episodes and cycle through the same process as before. Continue practicing until you can stay with the bodily discomfort and hurt with compassion and forgiveness, without judging (letting your judgmental thoughts come and then letting them drift away). This will take weeks, not days. The key is to stay on the path!

## Practice Patience When Anger Is Hot

In many of the preceding exercises, you imagined being angry but you were at home, probably alone in a room, and you brought on the anger experience deliberately. That is not how anger usually occurs. It flares up when you may not have expected it, catching you off guard. This is the toughest challenge: What do you do when the anger is hot, right there, raging inside of you?

One of the reasons why you practiced the previous exercises—and particularly the last one—is to prepare for those times when anger gets ignited quickly in real-life situations. Of course, you can bring any of the new skills you've been practicing into the moment when anger flares up. Yet in the heat of the moment it's sometimes difficult to remember what exactly you're supposed to do. So let's keep it simple: *Do nothing and practice patience.* Step back. If you can sit down at that moment, do so, and sit still with what you experience in that moment. Here are specific guidelines for what you can do:

- **Say and do nothing.** It may not feel like it, but you do have a choice here. You can do what your mind and body tell you to do. As in the past, everything's pushing you to act: you want to be right, and you want to straighten things out. You could do that—and what does your experience tell you about that choice? Or you can make a choice that seems as ridiculous and unnatural as pushing into the finger traps: you can choose to act with patience. You stop, shut up, sit still, and wait until the hardness of the stirring, raucous, and searing energy gradually softens and cools. You aren't suppressing here.

You're just honest with the fact that you're angry, or hurt, or sad, or lonely, or fearful, or whatever you're experiencing at the moment. And you stay with it, without feeding it or reacting to it.

■ **Watch the mind machine as an observer.** We guarantee that the mind machine will be in overdrive doing its blaming. Don't get tangled up in what it's doing; don't respond to it. Just watch what it's doing from the compassionate observer perspective, and practice gentle acceptance.

■ **Ride the tiger.** This is really tough. Sitting with the discomfort and doing nothing while you feel like exploding is like riding a wild horse or a wild tiger; it's very frightening. In that moment, bring attention to the physical experience of anger. Is there pressure? Is there tightness or contraction? Where, specifically, do you feel it? Does it have a shape? Observing your feelings will help you see them as separate from you.

Here, perhaps for the first time, you can make a choice to sit and stay with the juicy energy that you have for so long acted to push out of view. And you can do so in your daily life. Once you are still, you can bring compassion and curiosity to the energy and pain. Look deeply into your experience without attempting to resolve it, fight it, or suppress it, and without acting on it. Just let it be. As you look, see if you can find the pain. Once you locate the pain, as in the previous exercise, look more deeply behind it for something that you are attached to or that you are holding on to. The attachments will be different for everyone. If what you find seems too big, start with the little attachments that are also there.

Approach this act of patience with softness and curiosity. You do have a choice to hold on here or let go. This quality of patience is very much like the practice of extending forgiveness.

We mentioned resolution and relief earlier, and that whatever you do in anger will bring no relief. As you practice patience, you may very well find that letting go of your attachments and resentments can bring a sense of enormous relief, relaxation, and connection with the softness and tenderness of your heart. Patience breeds connection with others; anger does the opposite.

## Nurture Comfort in Your Own Skin

Emotional pain and hurt will show up in many areas of your life. The suggestions below are about further expanding your response-ability when faced with pain and hurt. Each builds on skills outlined in earlier exercises. All take you into your pain and discomfort, and help you develop comfort in your own skin. The payoff is this: Your emotional pain will no longer be fertile soil for your anger. It won't have the capacity to sidetrack you from moving in directions you care about. We suggest that you take the perspective of wise mind and compassionate witness for each exercise. They will help you choose to open up to and embrace these painful experiences when they show up and learn to bring compassion and forgiveness to them.

### Facing Your Fear

Start by making contact with the dangerous or painful thing you are afraid of. What is the nightmare or worst-case scenario? Notice the bodily sensations that accompany these thoughts. Be specific. You may fear being exposed as incompetent or being embarrassed, humiliated, criticized, or devalued. Or perhaps you fear the emotion of fear itself. The problem here is not the emotion, but what you do about it and how that action gets in the way of doing things you value. Adopt an observer perspective and watch your fear-related thoughts, worries, bodily sensations, and images. Separate them out using the wise mind technique, and stay with them. Don't try to resolve or fix them. Simply watch, as you've been practicing.

### Facing Guilt

Start by asking yourself this question: "What is the rule for how I am supposed to be or act that I violated when I started feeling guilty?" You may have one rule that emerges again and again (such as, I must never miss an appointment or fail to follow through with what I said I would do); or there may be other rules that get in the way of you moving in the direction of your values. As you contact these rules, notice the hard and rigid quality of each of them, the feeling that to break them is to be bad. Also notice how each rule stands in the way of something that's important to you. Now examine the rule for what it is. Does this rule come from your own experience? Is the rule life affirming? Has it worked for you? Is this rule getting in the way of something you cherish and hold dear? Within cultural boundaries, you need to decide whether following the rule is more important than what you value in this situation. Are you willing to let the rule go if that means doing what is important to you? If so, then let go and get going.

### Facing Loss and Grief

People run from grief because they resist pain and fear being overwhelmed by powerful feelings. This running, in turn, tends to be life constricting. Have you allowed yourself to grieve and experience the normal pain that goes along with loss? If not, you need to do just that. Your work here is to experience the pain of loss and then allow yourself to let it go. To do this, allow yourself about half an hour each day to reminisce, appreciate, and experience regret. At the same time, let in the feelings of sadness that come along with giving up the lost person or object. Trust that the waves of pain will pass before their intensity overwhelms your ability to stay with them.

### Facing Hurt

The active work of facing hurt is to acknowledge it—openly, directly, and honestly, without blame or accusation. Focus on what hurts and how that hurt is getting in the way of aspects of your life that are important to you. Focus on communicating the feelings of hurt directly to yourself and others who may have brought these feelings on. For instance, you might say "I feel hurt when you joke about my cooking." Don't look for apologies to resolve your hurt. Simply acknowledge it, bring compassion to it, and let it go with the gift of forgiveness. As with all the other exercises, doing it once will not be enough. You need to practice repeatedly. Over time, you will get better at facing your hurt with compassion.

### Facing Helplessness with Response-Ability

Many things in life occur outside of our control. It's vital that you detect the difference between what you can and can't control. As you learned in chapter 4, trying to meet uncontrollable circumstances with control only buys you frustration, anger, and a sense of helplessness. Feelings of helplessness almost universally redirect our attention from what we can control to what we cannot control. Acknowledge feeling stuck; then choose to be response-able. Focus on what you can control to have your needs met and to keep you moving forward in directions you care about. These are both things you can control and do something about. Be specific here: write down a plan that keeps you moving forward, even in the face of adversity.

### Feelings of Emptiness and Loneliness

Most people will go to great lengths to block feelings of emptiness and loneliness from their awareness. It's important here, as with the other painful emotions, to separate blame from the pain. You need to experience your own loneliness directly without linking it to the faults and failings of others. To encourage the feeling and to develop comfort with it, you could take a brief walk in a quiet place, sit alone for ten minutes with the TV and radio off, or resist the impulse to call someone to fill the void, and instead notice what it's like to postpone contact for ten minutes or so. These little exercises will make you aware of your loneliness; and, somewhat paradoxically, they may generate a sense of calm and inner peace. The most important element of these exercises is to notice and embrace what it feels like to be alone with yourself instead of running away from emptiness and loneliness and filling these voids with anger and blame.

# THE TAKE-HOME MESSAGE

Pain and hurt are facts of life so long as one is living. Anger and unforgiveness feed off unresolved pain and hurt. This is why we are showing you the pathway into your own pain and hurt, so that you can douse the fuel that drives your anger.

It's important to remember that facing pain and hurt is not about self-torture. As Pema Chödrön (2001) noted, staying with pain without loving-kindness is just warfare. This is why most of the exercises in this book have a soft and gentle, rather than a confrontational, quality to them. Self-compassion and courage are vital. By learning to develop compassion and loving-kindness for your experiences, rather than stuffing them or running away from them with anger and aggression, you are exercising control where you truly have it!

Become masterful at bringing compassion to your experiences—all of them. Then commit to extending compassion, forgiveness, and kindness to others, regardless of how they respond. This is about you and for you—forgiveness is the most courageous, honest, and loving gift you can give to yourself. Expect big changes as you work with these exercises, but don't expect changes overnight. Continue to work with the exercises daily. Stay committed to the practice. Stay on the path. The outcome will take care of itself.

---

## WEEK 9
### *Facing my hurt with forgiveness*

**Point to ponder:** Practicing forgiveness and patience are the most powerful antidotes to anger. They are for me, about me, and given by me.

**Questions to consider:** Am I willing to choose the path of forgiveness and extend kindness to myself and others? Am I willing to face my emotional hurt and pain with patience, compassion, and kindness so that I can move on with my life?

---

# Chapter 10

# Commit to Take Positive Action in Your Life

*Success is the ability to go from one failure to another with no loss of enthusiasm. Until you are committed, there is hesitancy, the chance to draw back, always ineffectiveness. The moment you definitely commit yourself, then providence moves, too. All sorts of things occur to help you that would never have otherwise occurred. Whatever you can do or dream you can do, begin it! Boldness has genius, power, and magic in it.*

—Sir Winston Churchill and W. H. Murray

Previous chapters provided you with fundamentally different ways to respond to your anger and hurt. You are now getting to a place where you've never been before. This place affords you more productive and vital options when faced with hurt. If your values are the compass points that guide you through your life's journey, then your goals are the road map that can lead you there (Hayes and Smith 2005). The next step is to take control of your actions and start moving in directions you want to go.

We'll help you put your values into action in ways that can profoundly change your life for the better. The wonderful thing about values is that you can live them. The key to living out your values is to break them down into incremental steps. You must commit yourself to taking those steps by setting goals and following through with action. Living a rich life is all about taking steps, however small or large, each and every day toward achieving your goals and living your values. By taking charge of your behavior, you take charge of your life.

Barriers are bound to show up as you journey out of your anger and hurt into the rest of your life. The risk of getting sidetracked by these barriers is great. So we'll also help you learn to move with the inevitable barriers that will spring up along the way, and how to approach setbacks and slip-ups with gentle forgiveness.

# SETTING AND ACHIEVING GOALS

Go back to the life compass you used in chapter 8 to explore your values. Now is the time to decide which of these values you want to start enacting in your life right now. Choose a value that is important to you and represents an area of your life that you have been putting on hold until now (you might choose one with a low action score). Perhaps you put this aspect of your life on hold because of anger-related barriers. If you sense that this is a domain where you're not yet ready to confront the barriers, choose a different one first.

At this point, we just want to walk you through one area to give you an idea of how the process works. Later you can go through the same steps for the other domains on your life compass. Once you've chosen a value, write it down on the top line of the values and goals worksheet that appears a bit later in this chapter. You may want to make several photocopies of this worksheet so that you have plenty of blank copies for other values that you will want to work on later.

Our colleagues Michael Addis and Chris Martell (2004) developed a behavioral program with six manageable steps for achieving goals. Let's go over them one by one:

1. Clearly define the goal.

2. Identify the steps necessary to achieve the goal.

3. Arrange the steps in a logical order.

4. Make a commitment to each step.

5. Take each step, no matter how you feel.

6. Pat yourself on the back after you complete each step.

## Identify Concrete and Achievable Goals

As you start thinking about goals, you'll find that some are short-term goals you can attain in the near future. Others are long-term goals you'll only be able to attain further down the road. Both types of goals are important, and achieving one may lead you to the next.

For instance, suppose you value your health and want to increase your fitness level. So, you commit to walking each day. Your long-term goal might be to walk to a telephone pole one mile up the road from where you live. Between your house and that pole are a number of other poles all spaced about the same distance apart. A short-term goal here might be getting to the first pole. The next day you commit to getting to both the first and the second pole, and so on. Ultimately, you need to go past all the intermediary poles to reach the long-term goal of reaching your one-mile marker. This is how short- and long-term goals work—they get you moving on a valued path.

In the space below (or on a separate sheet of paper), write down some goals related to the first value you chose on your life compass:

_____

_____

_____

It's important that your goals meet certain criteria to avoid ending up on a dead-end street. Steven Hayes and Spencer Smith (2005) give some good advice in this regard:

Setting goals is all about workability. If you don't make your goals workable in the context of your life, it's unlikely you're going to get very far down the path of your values. Choose achievable, obtainable outcomes that can realistically fit with your life. Doing this makes it much more likely you'll actually be able to live your values every day. (p. 182)

We suggest that you start with up to three goals. One of those goals should be a short-term goal—something you can start working on this week. Ask the following questions for each goal to make sure it's achievable:

- Is the goal concrete, practical, and realistic?

- Is it obtainable (something I can do and have control over)?

- Does it work with my current life situation?

- Does this goal lead me in the direction of my value?

If you can answer yes to all of these questions for a goal, write it into the left-hand column of the values and goals worksheet later in this chapter. If necessary, revise and clarify the goal until you get a yes answer to each question.

## Identify Steps and Arrange Them in Logical Order

Having settled on goals, you've put the first guideposts on your road map. Now focus on the incremental steps you need to take to get you there. Start with the short-term goal and break it down into smaller intermediate steps. Think of each step you need to take to attain your goal. Then write them down in the space below (or on a separate piece of paper):

_____      _____

_____      _____

_____      _____

Now think about a logical order for the steps. What needs to happen first before the other steps can follow? If no particular order is necessary, then start with the easiest step. Copy the steps into the values and goals worksheet in the order in which they need to be completed. Put the first one at the top. You can go through the same procedure for other goals you've identified. Put them in logical order and write them on the worksheet. You may want to make a few photocopies of the worksheet first or use additional blank sheets if necessary.

Let's look at two examples. Say your goal is to change jobs and eventually become manager in a larger corporation rather than the small outfit you're currently working for. This goal, in turn, includes smaller specific actions such as checking relevant newspapers and Internet sites for postings of managerial jobs, networking with others in your field, updating your resume, setting up an informational interview at a company that interests you, and making a job application to a potential new employer.

For another example, let's say you want to work on spending more quality time with your spouse or partner. This goal may be approached via several steps, such as doing something once a week with your partner that you both enjoy such as going to a movie or the theater, dining out, going away for the weekend, or taking a bike ride together. It is important that you do these things regardless of how you feel at the moment.

## Make a Commitment and Take the Step

Now it's time to make a commitment to step number 1. Are you willing to accept whatever discomfort your mind and body will give you? Are you willing to commit to the values explored in chapter 8 and to the behavioral and life changes they imply? Are you ready to commit to following through?

If so, commit to a day and time to begin step 1. Tell someone else that you have done so. Then, no matter how you feel at that time, do it. This is all about action and doing something different with your life. Unless you take action, nothing will change, and you'll continue to get what you always got.

Write the date when you achieve each step. Put a gold star on the chart if you want to. Make sure to congratulate yourself; give yourself credit for what you've accomplished, no matter how small the step was. Review this worksheet frequently. It gives you valuable feedback on how you're progressing, and it will encourage you once you start checking off your goals.

## Values and Goals Worksheet

My Value: _____

| The goal I want to achieve | Steps toward achieving my goal | Barriers | Strategies | Date achieved |
|---|---|---|---|---|
| Goal 1: | 1. | | | |
| | 2. | | | |
| | 3. | | | |
| | 4. | | | |
| | 5. | | | |

| Goal 2: | 1. | | | |
|---|---|---|---|---|
| | 2. | | | |
| | 3. | | | |
| | 4. | | | |
| | 5. | | | |

Here's how Harry, a forty-four-year-old mechanic and father of three, completed a section of his values and goals worksheet.

## Values and Goals Worksheet

My Value:  *Being a good dad with my kids*

| The goal I want to achieve | Steps toward achieving my goal | Barriers | Strategies | Date achieved |
|---|---|---|---|---|
| Goal 1: Spend more time with my kids | 1. *Set aside time each day to spend with each of my three kids. Get a daily planner for time with kids and to remember important dates like birthdays, sporting events, family trips* | *Stress from work—hard for me to unwind and have time for myself during the week* | *Use the planner to make time for myself. Get up early to have some time alone* | |
| | 2. *Be available for the kids. Be around the house more often, especially on weekends* | *Old habits after work just plopping myself down in front of the TV with a beer* | *Tape the news. Keep the TV off after I get home, and watch TV once the kids are in bed* | |
| | 3. *Brainstorm fun activities that I can do with the kids— go swimming at the lake, go see a movie, go to the carnival, play flashlight tag, card games* | *Noise—kids yelling and screaming (I'd rather be alone)* | *Use a wise mind perspective when the kids are getting to me. Remind myself that kids are kids, and that I am responsible for what I do* | |
| | 4. *Practice patience with them. Work on enjoying the time with the kids for the sake of it* | *Anger—when they don't listen to me, I withdraw and want to be by myself* | *Use the calendar to remind myself of my values— having a good relationship with my kids as a dad* | |
| | 5. *Show them that I care about them—say "I love yous more"; give out more hugs, even when I don't feel like hugging; be willing to do what they want to do, even if that's not exactly what I want to do* | *So many things to do around the house after work* | *Try to involve the kids in some of the house projects—have them be my little helpers. A good way for me to teach them some skills and for us to spend time talking.* | |

## Moving with Barriers and Setbacks

As you embark on your journey of acceptance, putting your values into action, you will find the road to be full of barriers. Some barriers are external, such as lack of money, time, opportunity, physical space, geographical constraints, or even weather. You can work through some of these barriers by brainstorming alternatives and perhaps talking with a good friend about them to get some fresh ideas. Yet by far the most frequent and tricky barriers that you face are those nagging internal barriers that have also slowed you down in the past. These may be difficult anger-related thoughts, feelings, bodily sensations, or impulses.

That's what the previous chapters have mostly been about—getting you ready for all the moments when barriers are going to show up in the form of thoughts you've believed in, along with the pain, hurt, feelings, and sensations you've been trying to avoid. This is the time to employ some of the strategies you've learned in this book: the observer, mindfulness, and acceptance strategies. If you can't remember these, flip back through the book to remind you what they are and how to do them.

We are brought up to believe that when a barrier comes up, we should just get rid of it, overcome it. The problem with this strategy is that getting rid of and overcoming entails struggle. As you may have found out in the costs of anger exercise in chapter 2, this kind of struggling with your anger doesn't tend to work well. These are the times when you need to listen to and trust your experience, not your mind!

You don't need to overcome barriers on your road to living your values. The key is to accept and move *with* the barriers—take them along for the ride! You can deal with the obstacles, setbacks, and anger slip-ups you'll undoubtedly experience in the same way you deal with your evaluative mind and your anger feelings. You don't push them aside; instead, you make room for all the unwanted stuff that has been stopping you from doing what is best for you. You acknowledge that stuff, stay with it, watch it from the wise mind observer perspective, *and* keep on moving in the direction you want to go—all at the same time.

## DRIVING YOUR LIFE BUS

You can think of yourself as the driver of a bus called, "My Life." You're headed north toward your Value Mountain, [insert one of your values here]. Along the way, you pick up some unruly passengers, like these blaming, critical, anger-related thoughts that your mind comes up with. Other passengers on the bus traveling with you are the feelings of pain and hurt that you contacted in earlier exercises. These passengers are loud and persistent. They frighten and seemingly bully you as you drive along your chosen route.

After a while, you realize that when you turned around while trying to argue with these other passengers and calm them down, you missed a road sign and took a wrong turn. Now you find yourself about one hour out of your way, headed south. What do you do? You are, in a sense, lost, but you're not directionless. You could stop the bus and focus on getting your passengers in line. What would it cost you to do so? Thoughts and feelings cannot prevent you from turning your bus around and heading north again toward the mountain—unless you

Figure 3. "Taking the Bullies with You to Value Mountain" was conceptualized and illustrated by Dr. Joseph Ciarrochi and Dr. David Mercer, University of Wollongong, New South Wales, Australia. Reprinted with permission of the authors.

give them that power. If getting to the mountain is important to you, then what you need to do is stay in the driver's seat of the bus and keep on driving north toward the mountain, no matter how much noise those other passengers are making.

The uncomfortable passengers are still on the bus with you. You can't get rid of them. As you get back on the road to your Value Mountain, they creep forward and scream, "Pay attention to us! Turn around! Go back! Take this detour—it's safer, easier—it'll make you feel better." What will you do? Stopping won't get you to the mountain, and neither will the detour. Only you can take yourself to where you want to go—and you have no choice but to take the whole crowd with you.

Those passengers on your bus will grab every opportunity to steer you off course. They'll try to convince you that you don't feel like doing this anymore, that it's all too much, too difficult, not worth it . . . *and* you keep on moving north.

You are in control of your life bus. You control the steering wheel with your hands and the accelerator with your feet. You can't control what kinds of feelings, thoughts, or fears will ride along with you. But you can determine where you're going. *That* is what you truly can control.

## Don't Let the Mind Machine Trap You

The mind machine won't stop its chatter just because you've made a commitment to act with compassion. Sometimes you will fall short of being accepting. Your evaluative mind may scorn you: "Stop all this acceptance and forgiveness BS. You just can't do it. The only thing you should accept is that you're a failure at acceptance!" When your mind is throwing this and other curveballs at you, it's important not to get tangled up in all that chatter. This is just another example of your mind doing what minds do all the time: evaluate. It's just more "blah, blah, blah" from your mind.

Do you really need to argue with blah, blah, blah? Or can you make room for whatever your mind comes up with and let it be? This will free you up to move on with your life, no matter how strong or powerful the feelings are, no matter how loud the thoughts yell at you. These are the times when you need to watch and expose your mind machine in action as you've learned to do in previous exercises. The practice is always the same: you simply acknowledge and observe your mind's doings without struggling against or believing them. Instead of falling prey to a chain reaction of vilification of others, anger behavior, and self-scorn, you can gradually learn to drop all the story lines your mind is coming up with.

### Flexibility Creates Response-Ability

It's really important to be flexible when you encounter barriers. Look at Anna's situation. When all the Ivy League colleges she had applied to rejected her application, she felt sad and angry at all those "stuck-up admissions people." Her mind told her, "You have to go to an Ivy League school." She listened and ended up spending her time and money reapplying, getting rejected, reapplying, and so on. Anna ended up not going to any college for two more years. She'd allowed her feelings and her mind chatter to keep her from getting a college education—one of her valued goals—by rigidly insisting she had to go to an Ivy League school. She'd let her sadness, anger, and events that were mostly outside her control keep her from applying to state schools. The more flexible your behavior is when obstacles crop up, the greater your ability to respond with intention and in accordance with your values. Flexibility nurtures response-ability—and makes it ever more likely that you'll achieve your goals.

### Are You Moving Forward or Backward in Your Life?

Whenever you encounter barriers and you're unsure whether your planned action is good for you, ask yourself one simple question, "Is my response to this event, thought, feeling, worry, or bodily sensation moving me closer to or further away from where I want to go with my life?" Below are some variations of this crucial question:

■   If that thought (emotion, bodily state, memory) could give advice, would the advice point me forward in my life or keep me stuck?

■   What advice would the value of [insert a pertinent value here] give me right now?

■   What would I advise someone else or my child to do?

■   In what valued direction have my feet taken me when I listened to this advice?

■   What does my experience tell me about this solution? And what do I trust more, my mind and feelings, or my experience?

Asking questions like these when faced with adversity and doubt is far more helpful than listening to what your unwise anger mind comes up with, or what the surging impulses seem to be telling you. The answers will remind you that past solutions have not worked. You now have the opportunity to choose to do something different, perhaps even radically different.

## Breaking Commitments and Recommitting to Action

Bringing compassion to your experience and practicing patience is difficult. When you make a commitment to an activity, or to practice compassion, it's important that you have a clear understanding of what commitment means. We're pretty sure that the passengers on your bus are going to be yelling and screaming at you, "You'll never make it!" "You'll just make a fool of yourself!" "You're going to get hurt!" Knowing that you're bound to experience discomfort and doubt, are you still willing to commit to this activity 100 percent and go through with it? Remember, commitment is not something you can merely try or do halfway. You either make the commitment or you don't.

We're not asking you to commit to a particular result or outcome ("being in a steady relationship by July 1" or "feeling better and less angry"). Particular outcomes are beyond your control. We're only asking whether you're willing to commit to doing something that will work for you *and* take all those passengers with you on your life bus. Will you do that and mean it?

The commitment is that you fully intend to follow through, not that you never fall short. In fact, we predict that you will fall short at some point. Your commitment is that if and when you do break a commitment, you will recommit and mean it once again. You will do whatever you can to stay on the path of commitment, moving in the direction of your values.

Choice and action determine how we deal with barriers and setbacks. At times, every one of us fails to live consistently with our values. Yet, every day we can make a renewed commitment to take actions that move us in life directions that we care about. A barrier or an anger slip-up does not mean that anger will take over your life again—unless *you* allow that to happen. It's your choice to either give up or recommit to small actions that make your life meaningful—and then put those actions into practice. So long as you do that and keep moving, you will be truly living a life that expresses your values. Our aim in this book is to help you make choices—every day and every moment of your life—that will keep you moving in the direction of those values.

# PRACTICE ACTS OF TLC AND KINDNESS

Being kind to yourself and others is also a value—and it's directly related to anger. Anger and kindness are two opposing forces. When one shows up, the other gets pushed aside. Practicing acts of kindness toward yourself and others is a behavioral antidote to anger. It's a simple thing you can do to bring peace and joy to your life. Be mindful that you may not always get kindness in return. The point is that you are taking charge by being kind. This is something you *can* do, regardless of the outcome.

## How to Be Kind to Yourself

Perhaps you'd like to be kinder to yourself, but you don't know how to start. We suggest that you begin by making a commitment to practice at least one act of kindness toward yourself every day. Start each day with this commitment. Think about something you could do to be kind to yourself. These acts are particularly important when what we call "TLC" issues arise—when you feel Tired or stressed, Lonely, and Craving (for example, for food, stimulation, nurturing, or praise). Our experience shows that at least 50 percent of all anger episodes are in some way associated with TLC problems. When people are irritable and needy, anger is easily provoked.

You can attend to TLC problems by nurturing Tender Loving Care toward yourself. This might involve taking time to practice meditation, reading a good book, going for a walk, listening to music, gardening, or preparing a good meal. Being kind can also include practicing acceptance and compassion toward your own feelings, memories, and hurts. You could give yourself the kindness of your mother's hand, as we described in chapter 6.

Valued living and being kind to yourself are related. Whenever you do something that moves you closer to one of your values, you're also being kind to yourself. Return to your life compass in chapter 8 and the values and goals worksheet in this chapter, and identify something you can do, however small, in the service of one of those values. Then commit yourself to doing it. Make giving yourself TLC every day a priority.

## Put Kindness Toward Others into Action

Be mindful of any chance you get throughout your day to act in a kind and compassionate way toward others. These acts of kindness could take many forms. You might practice saying, "please," "thank you," and "you're welcome" more often. You might open a door for someone or offer a helping hand. You could let a driver merge into traffic instead of making it impossible for them to do so. You could extend a smile to a stranger. Give a hug or a kiss to a loved one. Convey understanding, compassion, and forgiveness when you feel hurt, anger, and the urge to strike back.

The point of these activities and other random acts of kindness is that you are doing something positive and personally uplifting for the sake of doing so—"just because." You are expressing the value of kindness and compassion. Doing so may feel contrived at first, but don't let this feeling get in the way of your commitment to acting kindly. You need not feel peaceful and loving first to act in a kind and loving way. You can just do it regardless of what you feel.

With practice, acts of kindness will become automatic and bring with them an increased sense of peace, love, and trust. You'll find that people will be more likely to gravitate in your direction when you practice acts of kindness. This outcome can only enrich your relationships.

Regardless of the target or the outcome, kindness is fundamentally about you! Nurture it. Develop it. Make it the core of your being and how you choose to live.

## Make a Twenty-Four-Hour Commitment to Act with Compassion

We're not suggesting that you make a commitment not to feel hurt or anger. "I won't get angry today" makes no sense, because you can't control whether you feel angry. What we are suggesting is that you make a commitment to act with compassion toward yourself and others by acting in a caring and loving way. Remember that compassion is not a feeling. It consists of many acts of kindness and caring for yourself and others. Write this commitment down on paper; or, better yet, share it with someone you care about. Here's how to make it work:

- **Tell people.** Share with every significant person in your life that you are 100 percent committed to behaving in a loving and compassionate way between [time] and [time]. Explain that this means that you won't shout at, swear, hit, blame, attack, or denigrate anyone (including yourself). No exceptions or excuses. Let them know that you're going to be on your guard for disagreeable, aggressive behavior throughout this day as part of your commitment to make compassion a regular part of your life.

- **Decide what you can do and are willing to do.** Compassion can take many forms. You'll need to decide on clearly visible acts of compassion for yourself and others that fundamentally go against the grain of your old patterns of acting with cynicism and anger. So think positive and brainstorm here. Acts of compassion need not cost one penny. They are free and can be freely given—a helping hand, smile, hug, kiss, or listening ear when you feel like striking back; kind words instead of gossip, sarcasm, or criticism; expressing gratitude and appreciation for what others have done; time alone with those you care about; taking time out for yourself to relax; or making time to practice the exercises in this book. Be creative. Do something positive and uplifting for yourself and those around you.

- **Ask for help.** There's a good chance that keeping this commitment won't be easy—especially if you experience frequent, unpredictable anger. It will probably feel a bit strange. Ask others to let you know when they notice your acts of compassion. Don't be seeking approval or kudos here. Just look for acknowledgment that you are doing what you intended to do. Also ask them to remind you when they notice you slip into old patterns of expressing your anger, either toward yourself or others. You could come up with a hand gesture or a code word to signal anger behavior.

## Practice Patience and Compassion One Day at a Time

Sitting still with your anger after it's been ignited is one of the toughest parts of practicing patience on a day-to-day basis. So is letting go of the internal dialog and struggle with yourself. Over time, you'll get more skilled—so long as you keep practicing loving-kindness toward your own slip-ups, limitations, and all-too-human inability to be perfect.

Begin each day with this commitment: "Today, to the best of my ability, I'm going to act with patience." In the evening, go back and examine your day with loving-kindness. Don't beat yourself up if your day ends up filled with the same old things you've always done. Instead, bring loving-kindness, compassion, humor, and forgiveness to your evaluation.

Compassion, softness, flexibility, and courage are vital. Recognize that you're only human, and that you're going to make mistakes and experience setbacks. You're never going to be able to be patient and accepting all the time; still, you keep moving in that direction, one day at a time. What matters is that you are taking steps to bring acceptance and compassion to yourself and your experiences. The small steps eventually add up. Sooner or later you'll find that loving-kindness and patience will become a habit in your life.

## Use the Energy of Anger

Pema Chödrön (2001) describes an intriguing way you can use the energy of anger constructively. Emotions typically proliferate through our internal dialog—that is, our evaluative thoughts. If you label those thoughts as "thinking" when you notice them, you may be able to sense the vital, pulsating energy beneath them. This energy underlies all of your emotional experience, and there is nothing wrong or harmful about it.

The challenge is to stay with this underlying energy—to experience it, leave it as it is, and, when possible, put it to good use. When anger arises uninvited, let go of your blaming, critical thoughts, and connect directly with the energy underlying it (as you learned to do in chapter 9). What remains is a *felt* experience rather than a subjective commentary on what is happening. If you feel, and can stay with, the energy in your body—neither acting it out nor suppressing it—you can harness it in the service of actions that will move you forward toward achieving your goals. The raw energy of anger is fuel. You get to choose how to use it.

## THE TAKE-HOME MESSAGE

To change your life, you'll need to commit yourself to changing what you do, pure and simple. Acceptance, compassion, and kindness are never more important than when you deal with barriers. In the past, you've probably shied away from the difficult feelings, unwanted thoughts, uncontrollable impulses, situations, people, and personal enemies that tend to trigger your anger. You can choose to continue to do that, and you know where that will lead you. Or you can choose to take a different path, one that you can travel on side by side with the best teacher you'll ever have:

> I must emphasize again that merely thinking that compassion, reason, and patience are good, will not be enough to develop them. We must wait for difficulties to arise and then attempt to practice these qualities. And who creates such opportunities? Not our friends, of course, but our enemies. They are the ones who give us the most trouble. So if we truly wish to learn, we should consider enemies to be our best teacher! (Dalai Lama 2003, p. 62)

## WEEK 10 *(and beyond)*
### *Putting my values into action*

**Points to ponder:** I can live my values *and* take my anger and my hurt—all of me—along for the ride. My greatest barriers are those that my mind creates. I need not let them stand in the way of where I wish to go with my life.

**Questions to consider:** How can I put my values into action every day? How can I best move with my barriers toward a valued life? Is what I am doing now moving me forward or backward in my life? Is what I am doing now what I want to be about?

# Further Readings, References, and Other Resources

Besides the materials we've used for writing this book, we're including suggested readings for learning more about the ACT approach to anger. We particularly recommend the book by Steve Hayes and Spencer Smith for more examples and suggestions on how to use ACT in your life. We also recommend the book by Pema Chödrön—a great source of strength, courage, and practical advice on how to approach anger with its most powerful antidotes, compassion and patience. Thich Nhat Hanh's book contains practical advice on transforming yourself through mindfulness and watering the positive seeds in yourself and others, while starving the negative seeds.

# FURTHER READING

Chödrön, P. 2001. *The Places That Scare You: A Guide to Fearlessness in Difficult Times.* Boston: Shambala Publications.

Hanh, T. N. 2001. *Anger: Wisdom for Cooling the Flames.* New York: Berkley Publishing Group.

Hayes, S. C., and S. Smith. 2005. *Get Out of Your Mind and into Your Life: The New Acceptance and Commitment Therapy Guide.* Oakland, Calif.: New Harbinger Publications.

McKay, M., P. D. Rogers, and J. McKay, J. 2003. *When Anger Hurts.* 2nd ed. Oakland, Calif.: New Harbinger Publications.

# REFERENCES

American Psychological Association. 2005. *Controlling Anger Before It Controls You.* APA Online, Public Affairs. Retrieved on August 9, 2005, from www.apa.org/pubinfo/anger.html.

Addis, M. E., and C. R. Martell. 2004. *Overcoming Depression One Step at a Time.* Oakland, Calif.: New Harbinger Publications.

Brantley, J. 2003. *Calming Your Anxious Mind.* Oakland, Calif.: New Harbinger Publications.

Bry, A. 1976. *How to Get Angry Without Feeling Guilty.* New York: New American Library.

Chödrön, P. 2001. *The Places That Scare You: A Guide to Fearlessness in Difficult Times.* Boston: Shambala Publications.

———. 2005. The answer to anger: The courage to do nothing. *Shambala Sun* 13(March):32-36.

Chodron, T. 2001. *Working with Anger.* Ithaca, N.Y.: Snow Lion Publications.

Dahl, J., K. G. Wilson, and A. Nilsson. 2004. Acceptance and Commitment Therapy and the treatment of persons at risk for long-term disability resulting from stress and pain symptoms: A preliminary randomized trial. *Behavior Therapy* 35:785-802.

Dalai Lama (Fourteenth), Tenzin Gyatso. 2003. A Dalai Lama treasury. *Shambala Sun* 11(September)63.

DeAngelis, T. 2003. When anger's a plus. *Monitor on Psychology* *34*(March):44-55.

Eifert, G. H., and M. Heffner. 2003. The effects of acceptance versus control contexts on avoidance of panic-related symptoms. *Journal of Behavior Therapy and Experimental Psychiatry* 34:293-312.

Friedman, H. S. 1992. *Hostility, Coping, and Health.* Washington, D.C.: American Psychological Association.

Hanh, T. N. 2001. *Anger: Wisdom for Cooling the Flames.* New York: Berkley Publishing Group.

Hayes, S. C ., J. Luoma, F. Bond, A. Masuda, and J. Lillis. (in press). Acceptance and Commitment Therapy: Model, processes, and outcomes. *Behaviour Research and Therapy.*

Hayes, S. C., and S. Smith. 2005. *Get Out of Your Mind and into Your Life: The New Acceptance and Commitment Therapy Guide.* Oakland, Calif.: New Harbinger Publications.

Hayes, S. C., K. D. Strosahl, and K. G. Wilson. 1999. *Acceptance and Commitment Therapy: An Experiential Approach to Behavior Change.* New York: Guilford Press.

Hokanson, J. E. 1970. Psychophysiological evaluation of the catharsis hypothesis. In E. I. Megargee and J. E. Hokanson (eds.), *The Dynamics of Aggression.* New York: Harper & Row.

Lerner, J. S., and D. Keltner. 2001. Fear, anger, and risk. *Journal of Personality and Social Psychology* 81:146-159.

McCullough, M. E., C. E. Thoresen, and K. I. Pargament. 2000. *Forgiveness: Theory, Research, and Practice.* New York: Guilford.

Purdon, C. 1999. Thought suppression and psychopathology. *Behaviour Research and Therapy,* *37*:1029-1054.

Siddle, R., F. Jones, F. Awenat. 2003. Group cognitive behavior therapy for anger: A pilot study. *Behavioural and Cognitive Psychotherapy* 31:69-83.

Smith, T. W., and L. Gallo. 1999. Hostility and cardiovascular reactivity during marital interaction. *Psychosomatic Medicine* 61:436-445.

Suarez, E. C., J. G. Lewis, and C. Kuhn. 2002. The relation of aggression, hostility, and anger to lipopolysaccharide-stimulated tumor necrosis factor (TNF) by blood monocytes from normal men. *Brain, Behavior, and Immunity* 16:675-684.

Tavris, C. 1989. *Anger: The Misunderstood Emotion* (rev. ed.). New York: Simon & Schuster.

Wegner, D. M. 1994. Ironic processes of mental control. *Psychological Review* 101:34-52.

# INTERNET RESOURCES

## ACT-Related Books and Materials

www.ACT-for-Anxiety-Disorders.com
 This Web site for our anxiety disorders book provides information on how to contact us, and additional information about our other ACT books and the ACT approach in general. We also provide information on our lectures and workshops.

www.acceptanceandmindfulness.com
 This Web site contains information on New Harbinger books, including some of our own, in which acceptance and mindfulness approaches are applied to a variety of life problems.

## Acceptance and Commitment Therapy

www.acceptanceandcommitmenttherapy.com
 This Web site has many useful resources for those interested in learning more about ACT, as well as those actively engaged in ACT research and application. There is also an extensive collection of research support (for instance, you can find updated lists of empirical studies on ACT—and many of them can be downloaded directly from the Web site).

## Bruderhof Forgiveness Guide

www.forgivenessguide.org/forgiveness/sites/index.htm?rs=0/62/-59
 This Web site contains several useful resources and links to sites that help you nurture and develop your capacity for forgiveness.

## Center for Mindfulness in Medicine, Health Care, and Society at UMASS Boston

www.umassmed.edu/cfm/

This is the Web site for the Center for Mindfulness in Medicine, Health Care, and Society. The center is dedicated to furthering the practice and integration of mindfulness in the lives of individuals, institutions, and society through a wide range of clinical, research, education, and outreach initiatives. One of these initiatives is the Stress Reduction Program—the oldest and largest mindfulness program in the country based at an academic medical center.

## Pema Chödrön

www.shambhala.org/teachers/pema/#

On this Web site, you'll find information about Pema Chödrön's teachings, additional exercises, and her forthcoming books and lectures.

**Georg H. Eifert, Ph.D.,** is professor and chair of the department of psychology at Chapman University in Orange, CA. He was ranked in the top thirty of *Researchers in Behavior Analysis and Therapy* in the 1990s and has authored over 100 publications on psychological causes and treatments of anxiety and other emotional disorders. He is a clinical fellow of the Behavior Therapy and Research Society, a member of numerous national and international psychological associations, and serves on several editorial boards of leading clinical psychology journals. He is also a licensed clinical psychologist.


**Matthew McKay, Ph.D.,** is a professor at the Wright Institute in Berkeley, CA. He is the author and coauthor of more than twenty-five books, including *The Relaxation and Stress Reduction Workbook, Thoughts and Feelings, Messages, When Anger Hurts, Self-Esteem* and *The Self-Esteem Guided Journal.* He received his Ph.D. in clinical psychology from the California School of Professional Psychology. In private practice, he specializes in the cognitive behavioral treatment of anxiety, anger, and depression.


**John P. Forsyth, Ph.D.,** is associate professor of psychology and director of the Anxiety Disorders Research Program in the Department of Psychology at the University at Albany, State University of New York. He has published numerous articles on acceptance and experiential avoidance and the role of emotion regulatory processes in human suffering. He has been doing basic and applied work related to acceptance and commitment therapy (ACT) for more than ten years. He is a clinical fellow of the Behavior Therapy and Research Society and a licensed clinical psychologist in New York. He serves on the editorial boards of several leading clinical psychology journals, and is associate editor of the *Journal of Behavior Therapy and Experimental Psychiatry.* He is coauthor of *Acceptance and Commitment Therapy for Anxiety Disorders.*

# Some Other
# New Harbinger Titles